lifemates

lifemates

by Dr. Dave and Jan Congo

a lover's guide for a lifetime relationship

Love. Honor. Cherish.
faithmarriage.com

Faith Marriage, an imprint of
Cook Communications, Colorado Springs, Colorado 80918
Cook Communications, Paris, Ontario, Canada
Kingsway Communications, Eastbourne, England

Other LifeMates titles currently available:
Dates for Mates, by Lisa Keyes and Debbie Black
They Call Me Mr. Romance, by Mike Keyes

Senior Editor: Janet Lee
Cover and Interior Design: Image Studios
Cover Photo: © FPG International/VCG

Printed in the United States of America.

1 2 3 4 5 6 7 8 9 10 Printing / Year 05 04 03 02 01
CIP data applied for

CONTENTS

INTRODUCTION

Married for All the Wrong Reasons!

We remember the fun we had setting up our little apartment in downtown Chicago and using our wedding gifts for the first time. Sharing those first few weeks of home-cooked meals as a married couple made us feel as if we were playing house. A few years ago we thought it would be great fun to pull out our old slides and revisit that apartment. We looked at three slides and begged each other to stop! That apartment was so plain and ordinary—which means our memories were rosier than reality. Somehow that newlywed stage had a glow to it. Even the bills that had to be paid, the work that had to be adjusted to, and the realities of graduate school seemed somehow brighter because we were together.

Close your eyes and remember the first month you were married. The wedding with all its festivities and the honeymoon with all its memories were behind you. You faced an unknown future with the person you love by your side. Together you were ready to set up house and settle down to the task of creating a life together—a married life. It was probably quite a change to go from all the attention—the showers, the parties, the wedding itself—to being just the two of you.

As time went on, and you learned what it was like to live on a daily basis with another human being, not just the person of your dreams. Perhaps a dark thought periodically passed through your mind. *Maybe I married too quickly. Maybe I married for the wrong reasons.* If you've had those fleeting thoughts, welcome to the club. After watching and counseling other couples for over twenty-five years, it is our perspective that most, if not all of us, married for the "wrong reasons."

Wrong Reasons

Some of us married in hopes of being taken care of, since others had always taken responsibility for our lives. Some of us got tired of carrying all the burdens of life as single persons, so we married to find some relief. For others, perhaps Mom and Dad's control seemed suffocating. It was as if our parents didn't want us to grow up and become our own person, so we used marriage to declare our independence.

Perhaps social pressure was behind your choice to marry. Your friends were engaged, married, even starting families, and you didn't want to be left out or feel like a third wheel. Maybe you experienced the "meat market" of the college and singles group social scene and were all too glad to escape that pressure with a "catch." (If you attended a Christian college, then you know what social pressure we're talking about. All it takes is one date before the tongues begin wagging. You're assumed to be a couple from that point on.)

Sexual attraction may have helped you choose marriage. You'd never experienced such strong feelings before. You could barely keep your hands off each other because the attraction was so intense, and you wondered if you would remain sexually abstinent before marriage. Some succumbed to sexual pressure and "jumped the gun." Perhaps there was a resulting pregnancy, and it seemed that the only honorable choice was to get married. Or perhaps you married a second time because you had an affair in your first marriage.

Some of us married our mates because they had qualities that we adored—qualities that we frankly didn't have. Somehow, in their arms we felt more attractive, more intelligent, more fun, and more alive. We felt more complete and less empty than we'd ever felt before. Often we gained the admiration of others as a result of our choice. We all loved being loved, feeling we were the apple of someone else's eye. We didn't necessarily know much about loving someone, but receiving love was great.

Or perhaps you were looking for someone who needed you desperately and made you feel strong, important, and invaluable. You hoped that with this person your loneliness would become a distant memory. You would belong to someone, someone who appreciated you and whom you could take care of. Maybe you even saw the person you were dating as your last chance. Better grab on, you decided, since no one else is likely to show up on the horizon.

Whatever your reason, on your wedding day you stood before your pastor, priest, rabbi, or justice of the peace and pledged yourself to each other. With those spoken vows, you became life mates.

Everything went along fine until that day when perhaps your husband or wife asked more of you than you were willing to give. In that dark moment of disillusionment you may have asked yourself, "Is it possible to create a lifetime love story with someone I married for all the wrong reasons?"

Our answer is "yes"—a resounding "yes," despite the fact that ninety-nine percent of us married for all the wrong reasons. Frankly, we're not even sure what the right reasons are. Lifetime marriages are not dependent on what happened or didn't happen in courtship.

Marriage Must Be Intentional

A lifetime love story is intentional. It is deliberate. It doesn't just happen by accident, but is the result of daily choice—a choice to look ahead and not back. Instead of saying, "Maybe I didn't," our words need to be, "Today I choose."

Naomi Remen, M. D. recounts the story of a former patient who, after being separated from his skiing buddies, spent three days in below-zero weather. Miraculously, he managed to survive, but he suffered severe frostbite and progressive gangrene in his feet.

Local surgeons wanted to amputate, but it was hoped that a renowned vascular surgical team could avoid this. They performed the operation and waited and watched. Slowly the young man's left foot began to improve, but his right one continued to deteriorate. Yet he refused to allow doctors to amputate.

The toxins from that foot began to flood into his body. His fiancé, family, friends, and medical staff tried to get him to change his mind. The doctors made it clear that his refusal to amputate was now threatening his life. His fiancé, after listening to one more request by the medical team to operate, became angry. She said, "Why don't you marry your foot? You can't have both of us." With that, she took off her sparkling diamond ring and put it on the black, rotting tissue of his toe. The young man said nothing. Everyone left the room.

The following day he scheduled surgery to amputate the rotting foot. After a successful surgery he was fitted with an artificial foot. He underwent rehabilitation and at the end of the year had only a slight limp.

Two weeks after his wedding, the surgeon asked him what had made him change his mind. He replied that his fiancée's action shocked him into reality. He saw that he'd been more attached to keeping his foot than to their future together. Yet when he'd been alone on that mountaintop in the snow, it was the thought of her love and their life together that had helped him survive.

In marriage as well as in life, our focus must be on what we're choosing rather than what we're losing. The apostle Paul's focus was dramatically redirected by his Damascus experience. He writes these words: "But one thing I do: Forgetting what is behind and straining toward what is ahead, I press on toward the goal to win the prize for which God has called me heavenward in Christ Jesus" (Philippians 3:13, 14). Like Paul, we need to embrace wholeheartedly the road on which we find ourselves.

Perhaps you married for all the wrong reasons. So what? This is now a moot point. You are married! This book, *Life Mates for a Lifetime: A Lover's Guide for a Lifetime Relationship*, is about choices—daily, deliberate choices. We will outline thirteen decisions that will grow us into people capable of being intimate companions on life's journey. These decisions have come from our own marriage journey and from the marriage stories of the hundreds of couples we have counseled. They all have their basis in God's Word, the Bible.

It is our belief that we as couples must become the change that we seek. Dreams that aren't followed by deliberate choices don't come true. Healthy marriages begin with commitment and are sustained by discipline. This creates opportunities for Jesus, our Savior, to mature us. Our part is to grapple with choices that don't necessarily come naturally.

When a pier juts out into the ocean, it is utterly at the mercy of the individual pilings on which is stands. Strike out one piling from beneath the pier, and the whole structure suffers a shock. The pier is weakened. Knock out several pilings, and the pier will collapse. Similarly every marriage juts out into a cultural sea, resting upon the pilings of both partners' choices. Every time a decision is ignored or reneged on, the marriage suffers a severe thunder shock. No pier, and no marriage, can stand for long with one-fourth of its pilings gone or damaged. Every piling, every decision, is crucially important.

It's No Accident

Healthy marriages don't happen by accident. The tendency of nature is toward the wilderness. If our marriage isn't getting healthier, then it's dying. Each of us would benefit from a daily recommitment to the thirteen decisions discussed in this book. If you and your husband or wife make these decisions conscious, if you get the fundamentals down, it is our belief that together you can weather any storm. You can find life and love on the other side of a desperate situation. Choosing these thirteen non-negotiables in the ordinary moments of life will result in proper preparation for the moments of crisis. As legendary Packers coach Vince Lombardi said, "We play the way we practice."

It is our prayer that you will find encouragement and challenge, grace and truth in these pages. Perhaps some of you, after reading this book, will say, "We've made these choices, and we will continue to make them even though we didn't know what we were really doing." Great! Rejoice in the strength of the relationship you have built. Others of you may discover that you've made most of these decisions, but perhaps there are one or two that you need to reconsider. And some of you will discover that the absence of intentional choice in your relationship is one of the primary reasons you feel so lost.

Ideally, these thirteen decisions will be made by both of you, as husband and wife. If so, health and vibrancy will flow into your relationship. But if you find yourself in a marriage where you are the only one willing to be intentional about making these choices, don't lose heart. These decisions will strengthen your character and move you towards maturity. And who knows how God might use your faithfulness to bring change into your spouse's life?

When this book goes to print, we will have celebrated our thirtieth wedding anniversary. Please know, however, that we don't have a "perfect" relationship anymore than do the couples introduced in these pages. Perfection is not our goal, love is. We've already planned what we'll say to each other and to our family and friends at our fiftieth wedding anniversary celebration: "We married for all the wrong reasons, and you know what . . . we'd do it again!"

DECISION ONE

"I Will Lock the Escape Hatch and Throw Away the Key"

Jan recalls: It had been one of those days in the counseling office. Dave and I looked at each other. Exhaustion seemed to be coming out of every pore. We both felt heavy in our spirits.

I studied the verse I had framed on my wall: "I would have lost heart, unless I had believed that I would see the goodness of the Lord in the land of the living" (Psalm 27:13, NKJV). Below the verse were some thoughts I had penned one day.

> As a therapist, I would have lost heart in the face of men's cruelty to women and of women's cruelty to men. I would have lost hope in the face of marriages that seemed to be crumbling. I would have lost love in the face of incest and abuse. I would have lost peace in the face of personal disintegration. But I believed that I would see the goodness of the Lord in the land of the living. I didn't lose anything! Help me see Your goodness today, Lord.

"We love because it is the only true adventure."

Dave had been standing beside me, also focused on those

words. He put his arms around me and suggested that we place the dear couples we had counseled that day into God's care. Together we prayed that they could sense God's presence, that they wouldn't lose heart, and that our counsel would be one of truth, encouragement, and hope to them.

As we quieted ourselves with a cup of tea and some soft music, we made the comment to each other that all of these couples had failed to make a fundamental choice, and instead were trying to find a way to escape their problems.

Phil and Reba, a Christian couple, had been the first to walk through the doors of our office. They'd been married fifteen years and had three beautiful children. Reba was frightened because Phil told her that he just didn't have any feelings for her anymore. This caused Reba to say, "I think he's been planning to leave since our honeymoon." She admitted that they had become very isolated in the last five years. Everything else had become more important than their time together—the kids' sports, her parents' failing health, even church activities. Their physical intimacy had dwindled significantly to only three times in the past year.

Phil's preoccupation with his feelings had led him to question if he'd ever really loved her to begin with. After all, Reba was pregnant when they got married. He confessed to feeling forced to enter the marriage. He knew that God hated divorce, but he also had been blessed by a visiting speaker's message on grace on the previous Sunday. God would forgive him, he was sure. Phil wanted us to understand that he wouldn't think of divorcing his children, only his wife. He kept saying, "God will understand. He doesn't expect me to be miserable all the time. Anyway, Reba ISN'T fulfilling her duties as a wife. Nobody could live with her. I should have left a long time ago. I'm out of here."

Simone came to her session by herself. She really didn't know how she could have ended up in such a dead-end marriage. Her husband, a physician, was noncommunicative. When she'd greet him after a day, he'd barely mumble hello. Then he'd disappear into his home office and work on the computer for the rest of the evening. She knew he would never change. "What am I supposed to do?" she asked. "He is intolerable to live with. Life is too short to waste."

Simone badmouthed him to her parents and friends. She became the pitied victim. Her only interactions with her husband were about what he wasn't doing or wasn't providing for her. Every waking moment found her fantasizing about a dream lover. She had been a full-time mother for eight years, but she felt like a single mom. Her parents helped her with her kids because she was overwhelmed and incapable of doing the necessary daily tasks. She asked us, "Since he isn't being a husband, do I have grounds for divorce? He certainly isn't living up to my expectations."

notes

Then Randy and Joyce came in to see us. This was a second marriage for both of them. Joyce was upset. She had just learned that Randy had married her without letting her know that he owed thousands of dollars in back support to his ex-wife. She discovered this when his ex-wife's attorney served him with a notice of an upcoming court date. She wondered if she had grounds for annulment.

Rather than admit his dishonesty, Randy was furious at Joyce's lack of support. He condemned her attitude and questioned her faith. If she were an understanding wife, she would see how unfair and unreasonable his ex was. Maybe he should serve her with divorce papers before she went to her pastor.

Mark and Judith arrived for their appointment a little late. Mark was upset because Judith wanted to go out with her friends on the weekend. These friends were all either single or divorced women from work who loved to go dancing together. Mark thought that Judith's friends were using her as a solution to their own loneliness. He admitted that he was threatened by her friendships and wanted to raise his concern in a setting where there was some accountability. He was afraid that she was looking for someone new and might leave the marriage.

What we heard from each of these couples was a similar theme: hopelessness and despair. This caused them to look for a way out—a loophole. In each case, one partner felt if it weren't for that lousy spouse, he or she could go through life happy and fulfilled.

Each couple we saw, however, had failed to make the fundamental choice of "locking the escape hatch and throwing away the key." As a result, their energy was directed toward fantasy and escape. Self-examination and mutually acceptable solutions weren't even considered. Each person believed that his or her life would be 100 percent improved if only the other person would change. Since change was not forthcoming, divorce seemed an acceptable option.

Happily Ever After?

Society encourages us to keep our options open at all costs. All we have to do is open a *People* magazine to read comments like these: "I couldn't breathe, so I had to come up for air." "I'm thin, I have money. I want to play. I don't want to be tied down." "We're just two people going in two different directions." People question whether the long-term perspective itself isn't a fairy tale. We're told that if the marriage is too unpleasant, too mundane, too difficult, or too inconvenient, we should call it quits. Split the sheets. The prevailing attitude seems to be "Why go through the pain?" Marriage is perceived as a contract with an escape clause.

Commitment that is not personally convenient is not popular in this day and age. "Happily ever after" has been transformed into "Make me happy, or I'll find someone who will." In order to pursue our dream of "happily ever after," we trash our mates. If only we could trash the unrealistic dream instead. Keeping one's commitment has become an optional thing. The tragic results are insecurity, immaturity, an erosion of trust, broken homes, and broken hearts.

Susan found herself devastated by her husband Paul's choices. She sat in our office wiping away the tears of disillusionment as she shared how his attitude had affected her. She confessed that in the last few years she had stopped speaking up out of fear that he would react poorly and leave her. If she expressed a differing perspective, her husband's attitude suggested that their marriage was on the line. He threatened to leave her on a regular basis, and he was always comparing her to women at the office who were more attractive, more intelligent, or superior in some way or another.

This caused her to live in a constant state of stress and anxiety. The only peace came when she retreated into a fantasy life in which she imagined what love and acceptance would be like. Paul's

> This short-term attitude has led to a crisis of the heart. We have become a nation of throw away marriages.

lack of commitment always gave him the upper hand in their marriage, according to her. But what good was "the upper hand" when their marriage would have benefited if only they had joined hands? Now her worst fears had come true. He had walked out.

Perhaps you have experienced the devastation of a divorce. You can give testimony to the pain caused by broken commitments. In no way do we want you to feel judged or condemned. Instead, we are challenging anyone who is currently married to lock the escape hatch and throw away the key.

Real Commitment

As Christians, we are called to be countercultural, as this passage from Romans suggests: "Don't become so well-adjusted to your culture that you fit into it without even thinking. Instead, fix your attention on God. You'll be changed from the inside out. Readily recognize what He wants from you, and quickly respond to it. Unlike the culture around you, always dragging you down to its level of immaturity, God brings the best out of you, develops well-formed maturity in you" (Romans 12:2, *The Message*).

Did you happen to watch the 2000 U.S. Open Women's tennis semifinal between Venus Williams and Martina Hingis? Late in the match, Venus stood three points away from elimination when she made another mistake. Her father and coach, Richard Williams, had seen enough. He bolted out of his courtside seat, walked briskly upstairs through a tunnel, and out of Arthur Ashe Stadium. He kept right on going until he exited the grounds of the U.S. National Tennis Center, cursing a reporter as he left. Mr. Williams abandoned his daughter when she wasn't performing to his satisfaction. Little did he know that she would rebound to win that match and, two days later, the U.S. Open.

In contrast, God is committed to us regardless of how we are performing. Consider these verses.

"No one can snatch them out of my hand" (John 10:28).

"Know therefore that the Lord your God is God; he is the faithful God, keeping his covenant of love to a thousand generations of those who love him and keep his commands" (Deuteronomy 7:9).

"If you are faithless, I will remain faithful for I cannot disown myself" (2 Timothy 2:13).

"Come to me, I will be your God. You will be the children of my heart. I will betroth you to me forever in faithfulness and love" (Hosea 2:19-20).

God says that He will commit to us forever. He is going the distance with each of us. He doesn't just put up with us—He commits to us with both faithfulness and love. He is in this relationship with His entire heart for the long haul. God is committed to us

notes

no matter how we are performing, whether we are succeeding or failing.

This is no lightweight commitment. And just as God has made an unconditional covenant with us, He calls us to make such a commitment in our marriages. When we express our vows to each other and before the Lord, we are adopting the long-range view. We take on the identity of marriage. It is who we are. Then divorce is out of the question.

God has made a long-term commitment to His people.
God has promised.
God is faithful to keep His promise.
He sealed that promise with His blood.
He put His life on the line for that promise.
He is our Master. He is our Mentor.
God doesn't break His promises.
God keeps His word.
God has been faithful to me.
I choose to be faithful to my spouse.
I keep my word.

The Crack in the Wall

A mysterious crack appeared on the wall of the forty-second floor in a gigantic skyscraper. The manager of the building immediately sent for the architect who had designed the building. When the manager was informed that the architect had arrived, he went up to the forty-second floor to meet him, but the architect was nowhere to be found. Eventually he was located in the sixth-floor basement.

"What are you doing down here?" demanded the manager. "We have a serious crack on the forty-second floor that needs immediate investigation."

"Sir, you may have a crack on the forty-second floor, but the forty-second floor is not where your problem is," replied the architect. "Your problem is here in the basement."

"How's that?"

"It seems that a security guard employed in the building wanted to build a garage onto his house, but he was short of materials and money. So every night before leaving work, he took an elevator to the sixth-floor basement, chiseled one brick out of the wall, placed it in his lunchbox, and took it home. After six years, a crack appeared on the forty-second floor."

We know that is just a story. But in the same way, if a lifelong commitment is not the foundation on which we build our marriage, then it won't be long until cracks appear in our relationship. A marriage can only be as healthy as the commitment on which it is founded. If the foundation of a house is unstable, it is impossible for the house itself to stand firm and strong. Our marriage is based on an underlying covenant that we each renegotiate on a regular basis.

Marriage is not a perpetual joy ride. Have you discovered that yet? It takes an enormous expenditure of energy, courage, and determination. A relationship gains strength when it is stretched to the breaking point and doesn't break. The long-term perspective helps us endure and sustain the inevitable rigors, struggles, and challenges of life.

Marriage is not "going steady." It is going "till death do us part."

Author Philip Yancey attests, "Every human marriage has crisis times, moments of truth when one partner (or both) is tempted to give up. Older married couples will admit that during these times they questioned the entire relationship. Now, though, they retell the stories with humor and even nostalgia, for the crises fit together into—indeed, they helped form—a pattern of love and trust. Looking back from the vantage point of a few decades, it seems clear that the couple's mutual response to stormy times was what gave their marriage its enduring strength."[1]

> Commitment is the life principle of a meaningful existence. It is the critical decision that makes all other decisions possible.

Dr. Linda Waite and Dr. Maggie Gallagher state that eighty-six percent of couples who report being unhappy in their marriages but did not divorce were much happier and content with their marriages when reassessed five years later.[2]

Where there is a promise, there is a way!

You are saying to your beloved, "as long as I live I will be your man . . . your woman. I will be a key resource person in your life as long as we both shall live."

Marriage is the only public profession of unconditional love left in the world. On your wedding day, you are putting your conviction on the line and crossing it. You are unreservedly your beloved's. There are no loopholes and no conditions. You are dedicating your life to be a lover of your husband or wife with all that that entails. You take on being "married" as a huge part of your identity.

During World War II when the Americans hopscotched from island to island in the South Pacific, the marines risked their lives to establish a small beachhead on each island. After gaining a foothold, they would radio back that they had "taken the island." In reality, they had taken possession of only a very small portion of the island. They had yet to take the entire island. Their mission had just begun.

Similarly, the commitment you make on your wedding day is a general commitment. Your vows give permanence to your love and clearly define a boundary around your relationship. You are saying yes to anything that will promote and reaffirm your commitment and no to anything or anyone who will undermine your commitment. You are putting yourself on the line. There is no going back. You have established a small beachhead.

Yet every day you will gain a new understanding of the depth of this commitment. You promise to love, honor, and cherish your partner in every circumstance, crisis, and surprise that life hands you. You commit to work through whatever comes across your path. You set your mind to seek the other person's good whether you have warm feelings of love or whether you don't; whether you find yourself personally gratified by your choice or not.

Your commitment becomes more powerful than your moods or circumstances. Feelings may precede commitment, but once you make that commitment, feelings must take a backseat to it. The choice of commitment nurtures you in staying-power love. The love shared by two on their fiftieth wedding anniversary is a much deeper, mature love than wedding day love. Healthy marriages begin with commitment and are sustained through daily choices.

More than Feeling

O God
If You've taught us any one lesson
In our years of marriage
It is simply this:
Love is so much more than feeling.
Feelings—how they fluctuate!
Moods—how they vary!
We don't always feel cheerful
Or eager or assured.

Often we're frustrated
Even dismal and dumpy.
Work piles up
Deadlines bog us down
Dreams vanish like puffs of wind

Anxieties eat like acid.
But do we love each other?
Yes! Yes! Yes!
How do we know?
We know because despite
Our varying emotions
Despite our wounded egos
We've given ourselves
In a deliberate act of will
"Till death do us part."

That was our solemn commitment!
It is this very commitment
That forever sustains our love.
Thank you, God.
For a truth so deeply ingrained.
So wonderfully sustained.
—Ruth Harms Calkins[3]

"It is more noble to give yourself completely to one individual than to labor diligently for the salvation of the masses."
—Dag Hammarskjold

Developing a committed, deep, meaningful relationship with your spouse will require more love, humility, courage, and strength than any other task that life hands you.

Michael J. Peterson once had a song out on the country charts entitled "By the Book." One of the lines goes, "If I had lived by the book. . . . " A disc jockey interviewing Peterson asked him if the book he was referring to was the Bible. He said, "No, it was my wedding album. I wrote this song when we were having a particularly rough time in our marriage. When I looked back at my wedding album, it became obvious to me that if I had maintained the same attitude I had on my wedding day throughout my marriage, we wouldn't be in the predicament that we were at that time."

A commitment based on love limits our options but enlarges our life.

Then he continued, "That is when I decided that the "I do" I say every day is far more important than the "I do" said on my wedding day."

One couple we know keeps their written vows at the front of their weekly planners. They repeat their vows to each other on a weekly basis but pray through their vows daily, asking God to help them honor their promises. Another couple celebrates their wedding anniversary on a monthly basis. At that time, they recommit themselves to each other and to God by repeating their vows.

Another couple created a short statement that includes every promise from their marriage vows: "I will love you when times are good or bad. I will cherish you even when I am upset with you. I will honor you at all times. I will never be disloyal to you. And I mean this forever, so help me, God."[4] This statement became a morning ritual that repetitively reinforced their lifetime commitment to each other.

In what ways do you and your spouse demonstrate your commitment to one another? If you've never thought of it, and the thought appeals to you, then create a new tradition. In order to be intentional, we need to recommit to each other on a regular basis. Everything changes when we focus on our promise.

Bad News/Good News about Commitment

Bad news: It's not just about me anymore. I can't just come and

CAN "TILL DEATH DO US PART" BE CHANGED TO "SUBSTANTIAL PENALTY FOR EARLY WITHDRAWAL"?

go as I please. I now have to take another's needs and wishes into account.

Good news: I have a companion on life's journey. I'm not limited by my own smallness. I now can embrace another and I can be embraced. I will broaden my understanding of myself and of you.

Bad news: I don't get to do things my way all the time. I won't get to be in constant control.

Good news: I will learn self-control. I will learn that love always involves freedom.

Bad news: Living up close and personal exposes me to your dark side—your quirks, your faults, and your shortcomings. It also exposes me to my own. I no longer can pretend I'm perfect or that you're perfect.

Good news: I can learn to trust a love that really knows me. I don't have to fear that if I fail you, you will leave. I can learn to love an imperfect, unfinished human being.

Bad news: The two of us are no longer islands in a sea of love.

notes

We have to contend with the people in each other's worlds.

Good news: We get to contend with and perhaps be enriched by the significant people in each other's world. With that comes understanding, perspective, boundary setting, and sometimes empathy.

Bad news: When the road gets uncomfortable and full of potholes, I can't take another highway.

Good news: I have the opportunity to learn what it's like to be there. I can learn how to work things through. I will learn to value our strengths. I will discover that we can face the rocky and the uncomfortable and come out on the other side trusting our love and each other.

Bad news: I won't get to live a life free of conflict and frustration.

Good news: Frustration and conflict are a part of every life, single or married. These provide me with an opportunity to learn about myself, about you, and about our relationship.

Bad news: There will be times you will wish you were single.

Good news: These feelings will pass when you make daily choices that reaffirm your commitment and love. It won't be long until you find yourself rejoicing in your togetherness.

Bad news: Marriage will change me.

Good news: Life will change me. Marriage will give me an opportunity to grow up and to mature.

Bad news: Deepening intimacy takes time.

Good news: I have time. I have made a commitment to you for life. You have made the same commitment to me.

Commitment transforms both the person making the promise and the person receiving the promise. It is the life principle of a meaningful existence, the critical decision that makes all other decisions possible.

I need to lock the escape hatch and throw away the key. I will make a long-term commitment to my lover rather than adopting a short-term attitude.

I, _____, take thee, _____,
to be my wedded (wife/husband);
to have and to hold from this day forward,
for better, for worse,
for richer, for poorer,
in sickness and in health,
to love and to cherish,
till death do us part,
according to God's holy ordinance;
and therefore I pledge thee my love.

Decision #1
"I will lock the escape hatch and throw away the key."

For Reflection and Discussion

1. If you were to write out your personal short statement of commitment, what would it say?
2. In what ways do you demonstrate your commitment to your spouse? If you've never thought of it, and the thought appeals to you, create a new tradition.
3. Which of the following benefits of commitment mean the most to me?:

Character is developed in the long haul when we are faithful to the vows we have made, when we stay and work rather than running away.

> When we lock the hatch, fear dissipates, love prevails, and the way is opened for clear communication, empathy, and productive interdependence.

I learn to make promises and keep them.
I plug the leaks of indecision.
I am decisive.
I act based on principle rather than reacting on emotion or circumstance.
I increase my personal integrity.
My self-esteem grows.
I am a person of my word.
My enthusiasm is released.
My patience grows.
Short-term obstacles and resistance don't knock me off course.
I am to be trusted.
I learn to sacrifice for someone as Christ did.
I grow as a result of working through rather than running away.
I feel relief and new energy because
I'm off the fence.
I learn firsthand about unconditional love.
My direction is established.
My focus is fixed.
My fears are overpowered.
My hope and optimism are renewed.
I am obedient to Christ.

4. Ask your LifeMate which of the following benefits mean the most to him or her?

How commitment benefits my partner:

My partner:
feels confident in my love,
feels secure in my commitment.
knows he or she is chosen, and therefore, trust is deposited

in the emotional bank account of our love.
knows he or she can count on me to be there.
sees me as dependable.
feels safe, cared about, and celebrated.
feels free to be authentic with me.
feels as if he or she has a companion on life's journey.

notes

DECISION TWO

"I Will Be Intentional"

Marriage is full of mystery and uncertainty. Learning to live together, embracing the unexpected, wrestling with new issues, dealing with problems that arise—all this creates anxiety. Together we find ourselves in uncharted territory.

Anxiety and questions are close companions. Why is it that so many questions come in the dark of night? Can I do this? Will I let myself down? Can I be myself and still be married? Can we do this? Is our marriage big enough for two? How could my spouse possibly see things that way? Who is this person anyway? What in the world do we agree upon? Are we really dysfunctional? Do other couples struggle as much as we do? What's a healthy marriage about anyway? Is marriage supposed to be this hard? And so the questions continue.

Anxiety is extremely unsettling. It is normal to want to relieve these uncomfortable feelings as quickly as possible, so people often start searching outside of themselves for an answer. Many times in the counseling office our clients plead with us, "Just tell us what to do." People are looking for solutions.

The Love of Law

> There are two ways to slide easily through life: to believe everything or to doubt everything. Both save us from thinking.
> —Alfred Zorzybski

Many folks set out in search of a tried-and-true formula that will be guaranteed to work, such as "Ten Steps to the Perfect Marriage." They approach their families, their friends, their pastors, or their counselors for answers.

Linda went to see her therapist because her marriage had become a real challenge. As she was sharing her life story, she mentioned that when her husband proposed to her, he told her that God had told him that she was going to be his wife. Linda said, "I just went along with it. Was I going to argue with God? I guess I never really chose marriage."

Her therapist smiled. "Linda, you chose," he said. "You chose to let your husband choose."

Many women measure their husbands' performance as spiritual leaders by some standard of perfectionism that they have established.

Alice's best friend's husband, Joe, was an outgoing, charismatic Italian. He was enthusiastic about his faith. Alice's husband, Ken, certainly didn't have the same personality. He was a steady, quiet man. When he would initiate leadership in spiritual matters, Alice would block his every attempt. Her ridiculous expectations blocked her vision. She couldn't see her husband's attempts because she was trying to force him to fit Joe's pattern of spiritual leadership.

When we attempt to live by someone else's formula, we begin to disappear. Author Eric Fromm put it this way, "Today we come across individuals who behave like automatons, who do not know or understand themselves, and the only person that they know is the person they are supposed to be. Their meaningless chatter has replaced communicative speech, their synthetic smile has replaced genuine laughter, and their sense of dull despair has taken the place of genuine pain."[1]

We all choose. Even not choosing is making a choice.

The contemporaries of Jesus kept trying to get Him to live by the rules, to focus on the law. Why did Jesus allow his disciples to work on the Sabbath? How could He heal on the Sabbath? Did He believe in paying taxes to Caesar? How could He mingle with publicans and sinners? Jesus kept rocking their boat. He raised their anxiety.

The Law of Love

Jesus came to elevate the law into one great commandment—love. Rules create fearful submission, but God doesn't. God desires that we love Him with our whole mind, heart, and soul and our neighbor as ourselves. Jesus didn't impose a formula on anyone. He left room for choice and even rejection. God desires a "yes" to love. When His enemies couldn't compromise Christ's message, they killed Him!

Listen to how Philip Yancey describes it: "Throughout church history, Christian leaders have shown an impulse to pin everything down, to reduce behavior and doctrine to absolutes that could be answered on a true-false test. Significantly, I do not find this tendency in the Bible. Far from it, I find instead the mystery and uncertainty that characterize any relationship, especially a relationship between a perfect God and fallible human beings."[2]

The Law in Marriage

Dave says: When we started out on our marriage journey, we were trying to follow rules. Our pastor gave us a formula for a happy Christian marriage. We were taught in a convincing manner that in the biblical relationship, the husband serves God and the wife serves her husband. I wondered why I hadn't gotten married sooner. This sounded like a great formula. I found out that it was a formula all right—a formula for selfishness.

Jan adds: As for me, I tried very hard to follow this formula but feelings of anxiety started to boil inside of me. It was as if the life was slowly, "lovingly," being snuffed out of me. I saw that the only way to ensure a "happy" marriage was if I became Dave's Revised Standard Version, his clone. He believed that if I loved him, I wouldn't disagree. I would rubber-stamp his preferences. If I questioned anything, I was viewed as defiant and nonsubmissive. It was as if he had taken out a slip of ownership when he married me.

Dave: I hadn't really meant to become a married bachelor, but that is what happened. I was fresh out of seminary and wanted to prove myself. My life revolved around my ministry, and I wanted Jan's life to revolve around me. I had a subtle sense of entitlement. I believed that I was to be the only decision-maker in our family. "Just trust me, Jan," I would say. "I'll be kind about it. I'll consider your needs. Let me handle things. Don't give me any grief."

Jan: I tried to accommodate, but it became very obvious that my brain and my input were not welcome in our marriage. I stuffed my feelings as long as I could, but it all came to a head one weekend in the Rocky Mountains. We were at a retreat center with a number of couples from our church.

Dave: I was instructing the couples on how to have a wonderful marriage. I was letting them in on the secret formula. We came back to the room after my first talk. I sank into an easy chair, thinking what a fine job I had done and expecting some pats on the back from my dear wife. Instead, after she shut the door, she took her wedding ring off and whizzed it past my ear.

Jan: I said, "I've had it! I can't go on living like this. I'm a person too. If I disagree with you, I'm not your enemy, I'm just trying to give you my perspective. I'm tired of being treated like a child. I am not your clone. I'm an adult. I feel trapped and hopeless."

Dave: I couldn't figure out what had gotten into this godly woman, this pastor's wife. It didn't take a college degree to see that Jan was angry—very angry. But remember, this was only Friday night, and I had sessions to present on Saturday and Sunday. I didn't know if she was going to be walking the aisles with placards saying, "He is full of it. Don't believe a word he's saying."

Jan: Someone had to be the protagonist for change. This marriage formula had room for only one person: David. I was not leaving the marriage, since I had vowed before God to be in this marriage for life, but it was starting to seem like a life sentence. On that fateful day, I stopped being a "yes" woman. Unfortunately, anger blurred my vision and led to emotional reactivity.

Dave: I was really confused. Our problems had to be Jan's fault. I hadn't changed. Our marriage was smooth before she reacted. Each of us blamed the other for ruining our marriage and figured it was the other person's responsibility to see the folly of his or her ways. Our relationship was characterized by distance, blaming, selfishness, anger, power struggles, and loneliness. Even though we were married, we were emotionally divorced.

Then an opportunity opened up so that we could move to California for me to begin my doctoral studies at Rosemead Graduate School of Biola University.

As I got started in the doctoral program, I discovered that one of the requirements was that every graduate student needed to have two years of personal therapy. I couldn't believe it. My first thought was, "I'm not the one needing the therapy, she is!" I thought there must be some way to have Jan come in for a joint marital session. Then I could leave and let the therapist straighten her out.

That didn't happen! I had to have the therapy.

In session one day, the therapist stopped me in midsentence and said, "Dave, I've heard you complain about Jan and what she's not doing, how she's not fitting your formula for the godly wife, and how upset you are. David, what are you choosing to do to positively impact your marriage? What are you bringing to your relationship?"

Needless to say, I left the session unnerved but challenged. On the way out the door, he fired another zinger in my direction: "David, is your marriage big enough for two?"

Jan: Around the same time, I was part of an accountability group. These women didn't buckle in the face of my angry outbursts. They listened, they prayed, and they confronted me. Regardless of what David was doing, whom had I chosen to become? When I looked in the mirror, I had to admit that there was an angry, selfish, reactive woman looking back at me. I lacked self-control, and I had abdicated all personal responsibility in reaction to what I perceived as David's arrogance. It became obvious that Jesus wanted me to change regardless of whether my husband did or not. I needed to own my own stuff.

Believe me, there was nothing cozy about this time in our marital journey. The only good news was that we had stopped pointing the finger at each other. We stopped focusing on the speck in the other's eye and started owning the log in our own. Rather than living by someone else's formula, we started to search out who God wanted us to be. Instead of living reactively, we sought to live responsibly.

Letting Go of Law

Dave concludes: As we reminisce about the grief that we caused each other in the first eight years of our marriage, we have to acknowledge that we believed that there was a "right" and a "wrong" way to do marriage. Of course, each of us tended to see what he or she wanted as "right." Our preferences were moralized and spiritualized until we turned them into law. I could devalue what Jan wanted and make her look bad, and she could do the same to me. In that way, neither of us ever had to allow a spouse to influence us. We never had to grapple with issues and perhaps even adjust. Every selfish wish we claimed to be for the good of "us."

In our marriage it became very obvious that when we weren't willing to be intentional and make choices, we made rules. But marriage is diminished if it is reduced to a set of rules. Says Philip Yancey, "I cannot reduce my marriage to a formula. It is a living, growing relationship with another free being, very different from me and yet sharing much in common. No relationship has proved more challenging than marriage. I am tempted sometimes to wish for an "old-fashioned" marriage, in which roles and expectations are more clearly spelled out and need not always be negotiated. I sometimes yearn for an intervention from outside which would decisively change one of the characteristics that bring my wife and me pain. So far that has not happened. We wake up each day and continue the journey on ground that grows incrementally more solid with each step. Love works that way…."[3]

> "To know what you prefer instead of humbly saying 'Amen' to what the world tells you you ought to prefer is to have kept your soul alive."
> —Robert Louis Stevenson

Moving Toward Choice

Dreams that aren't followed by deliberate choices don't come true. In the long run, the choices we make shape our lives and our relationships. It is our choices that determine who we really are and of what we're made. Winston Churchill's words ring true: "We make our choices, and then our choices make us." Love rests on choice and action rather than on feelings.

A brilliant watercolor artist suffered a stroke. His right hand, his painting hand, was paralyzed. A dear friend visited him with fear and trembling. It took the artist a long while to get to the door and when he talked, his voice sounded like a recording that was played at the wrong speed. They spent the afternoon reminiscing.

Before leaving, the friend excused herself to go to the bathroom. When she returned she found the artist standing in front of his easel concentrating on a magnificent, unfinished oil painting. Her heart broke for the artist locked inside of him.

Then she watched as he picked up a paintbrush with his left hand. He then put it in his lifeless hand. With intense effort he trapped the brush between two fingers and rested the shaft against his palm. Then with his left hand guiding, he pushed the brush across the canvas, leaving a bright line of color.[4]

Choosing to courageously love one another is a little like that. None of us has any idea what life will bring across our path. Courage is accepting whatever it is and choosing on a daily basis to leave a bright, loving stroke on the canvas of your marriage, no matter what amount of effort it takes to follow through. Even if you are the only one choosing to exert effort.

Marital Styles

Just as the Lord created each of us as a unique human being, so each marriage reflects a blending of two people's uniqueness. Don't let anyone tell you that there is only one way to structure a healthy relationship. Together before God, you can create a marriage that satisfies and brings joy and security, rather than belong to a marriage that imitates or fits someone else's stereotype of what marriage "should be."

A few years ago two researchers, Judith Wallerstein and Sandra Blakeslee, designed a qualitative study of fifty couples who had built satisfying, lasting marriages.[5] The researchers' fascinating findings resulted from their sorting of these marriages into four distinguishable types. Some couples clearly belonged to one distinguishable type. Others were hybrids.

Each style gave priorities to some needs and relegated others to second place. Each provided a different degree and kind of closeness between partners. The view of roles was different in each type, as were the division of labor and the responsibility for child care. Each type could have a downside if the two mates let their relationship slide. At that point the negative possibilities began to dominate.

notes

1. **The romantic marriage.** Strengths: This couple feels destined to be together. This marriage has a lasting, passionately sexual core. Fifteen percent of the sample fell into this category. Downside: A self absorbed, childlike preoccupation with each other to the detriment of others in the couple's life.
2. **The rescue marriage.** Strengths: One or both partner's early life experiences were tramatic. Each person's individual healing and his or her ability to

give and receive love developed in the marriage. Twenty percent of the sample fell into this category. Downside: They reenact earlier traumatic experiences in their marriage.

3. **The companionate marriage.** Strengths: At its core are friendship, trust, and equality. Both partners work and they attempt to balance their emotional investment in the workplace with their emotional investment in the marriage and family. None of the couples married in the 1950s had "companionate" marriages. But 40 percent of those who married in the 1970s or later had this style of relationship. Downside: This marriage can degenerate into a business relationship or a "brother/sister" relationship.
4. **The traditional marriage.** Strengths: At its core is a clear division of roles and responsibilities. The man is the primary wage earner, and the woman is responsible for the home and family. Traditional marriage has changed in recent decades; the most important innovation is the division of adult life, especially for women, into many chapters. Stay-at-home motherhood is viewed as the first chapter. Many then reenter the work force at midlife after their children are grown, which is another chapter. In the study, all those who married during the 1950s and early 1960s and 25 percent of those who married in the 1970s and beyond had this style of relationship. Downside: When the children in these homes leave, often the couple has nothing in common.

In the past twenty-five years of counseling, we have been amused and amazed by the different styles of marriage or combinations of styles that couples create together over the lifetime of a marital relationship. Each mate's personality and value system seem to blend into the couple's own unique style of relationship.

We certainly have encountered each of the styles defined by Wallerstein and Blakeslee. In addition, we have created our own understanding of different couple's styles based on their decision-making:

1. Hierarchial Relationship. These couples choose one person to be the decision maker in the relationship. He or she makes decisions around children and parenting, sexual activity, family and friends, finances and religious orientation. The other partner's role is to be one of support and agreement—rubber-stamping the decision. If both mates are content with this arrangement, it works extremely well.

2. Unhealthy Hierarchy. If at any point, however, the supportive mate wants to question his or her LifeMate's decisions, the entire relationship is threatened. As a couple, they have developed few skills for sharing feelings, communicating or resolving differences. If the decision-maker decides to force his or her way on the other partner, this style becomes an unhealthy hierarchy with one partner playing the subordinate role. Only one person is usually satisfied with this unhealthy style—the decision-maker.

3. Isolated Relationship. These couples live under the same roof, but they live isolated emotionally. They are caught up in competitive lives. Each makes decisions which affect the other, but there is little connection and communication.

We encountered an extreme example of this style in a wealthy young couple whose motto was, "whoever does the payin' does the sayin'." If one of them decided to redecorate the house, the one paying for it would make the changes without consulting his or her mate. If the changes weren't appreciated the other mate could redo the job with his or her own money. Neither felt compelled to consider the needs and wants of the other.

Interestingly, if a couple has experienced misery in the unhealthy hierarchy style of marriage, then the isolated style seems to be their next style of choice. At least in the isolated relationship, there is room for two decision-makers. The isolated relationship couple just hasn't learned how to connect. They are afraid that connecting means control and a loss of their freedom. The question seems to be, "Can I be me and still be in this relationship?"

Therefore, they spend a great deal of time fighting what they perceive as control.

4. Partnership Relationship. These couples have multiple strengths including communication, spirituality, and a spirit of cooperation. They are committed to working differences through to resolution. They have an egalitarian role pattern, and see themselves as a team. Their marriage is big enough for two. They submit to each other's leadership when their LifeMate has more experience or expertise in an area. Because they both feel valuable to the relationship and respected by their LifeMate, they have strong sexual feelings for each other. They report high satisfaction with their relationship.

As a couple today, you get to try on different styles to see what works best for your situation. Together, you can create a marriage that gives God glory and brings fulfillment to both parties. You'll have to go through the tunnel of anxiety, conflict, discussion, prayer, and study to arrive at the destination that best fits the two of you, but you can intentionally create a marriage that gives God and yourselves pleasure. Don't let any other human being determine the rules for your relationship.

Choosing To Love

I married a man I respect;
I have no need to bow and defer.
I married a man I adore and admire.
I don't need to be handed a list entitled
"How to Build His Ego"
or "The Male Need for Affirmation."
Love, worship, loyalty, trust—these are inside me.
They motivate my actions.
To reduce them to rules destroys my motivation.
I choose to serve him to enjoy him.

We choose to live together and grow together,
to stretch our capacities for love even when it hurts
and looks like conflict.
We choose to learn to know each other as real people,
as two unique individuals unlike any other two.
Our marriage is a commitment to love;
to belong to each other to know and understand to care
to share ourselves our goals, interests, desires, needs
Out of that commitment the actions follow.
Love defines our behavior and our way of living together.
And since we fail to meet not only the demands
of standards but also the simple
requirements of love,
We are forced to believe in forgiveness
. . . and grace.
—Jerry and Barbara Cook [6]

Choice Determines Character

All the moments of marriage reveal whether we've fostered our character or forgotten about it. It should be obvious from our marriage story that as long as we were trying to fit someone else's formula, we forgot about developing our own character.

Marriage is our last best chance to grow up.
—Joseph Barth

We can't will ourselves into maturity, but we can adjust and align with what Christ challenges each of us to become. Marriage is guaranteed to expose our "natural" tendencies. But God is more interested in relationships than rules. He wants to use our marriage and our subsequent choices in our marriage to transform us and shape our character.

Choice # 2
"I Will Be Intentional"

For Reflection and Discussion

1. Look through this list of character traits and identify the areas in which you need to be transformed. Make the relevant Scriptures a focus of your prayer time, giving God complete freedom to change you from the inside out. As you tackle the hard choices, commit to character growth and stay with it. God's love will do its transforming work. What starts as an unnatural choice will eventually become a habit.

Lack of love	1 John 4:7-8,20; John 15:12	Love
Doubt	1 Thess. 5:24; Heb. 11:1	Faith
Worry	Matt. 6:25-32; 1 Pet. 5:7	Trust
Lack of rejoicing	Phil. 4:41; Thess. 5:16	Rejoicing
Hypocrisy	Job 8:13; Eph. 4:25	Honesty
Complacency	James 4:17; Col. 3:23	Diligence
Evil thoughts	Prov. 23:6-7; Phil. 4:8	Positive thoughts
Profanity	Ps. 109:17; 1 Tim. 4:12	Edification
Lying	Eph. 4:25; Zech. 8:16	Speaking Truth
Gossip	1Tim. 5:13; Rom. 14:19	Positive Speech
Hatred	Matt. 5:21-22; 1 Cor. 13:3	Kindness, Love
Wrath	James 1:19-20; Gal. 5:22-23	Self-control
Losing temper	Prov. 16:32; Rom. 5:3-4	Self-control
Jealousy	Prov. 27:41; Cor. 13:4-5	Preferring others
Complaining	Jude 15-16; Heb. 13:5, 15	Contentment
Murmuring	Prov. 19:31; Cor. 10:10	Gratefulness
Discontent	Phil. 4:11-13; Heb. 13:5	Satisfaction
Impatience	James 1:2-4; Luke 21:19	Patience
Ungratefulness	Rom. 1:21; Eph. 5:20	Thankfulness
Conceit	1 Tim. 3:6; James 4:6	Humility
Pride	1 Cor. 4:7; Prov. 27:2	Humility
Unforgiveness	Mark 11:25; Matt. 6:14	Forgiveness
Judging	Matt. 7:1-2; John 8:7-9;15:22	Self-examination
Bitterness	Heb. 12:15; Col. 3:12	Tenderheartedness

2. Which of the styles of marriage or what combination of the styles identified in this chapter would you say describes your marriage? Why do you think it fits? Do aspects of other styles appeal to you? Discuss these questions with your spouse.

3. We believe that every couple needs to intentionally choose their style of marriage and the habits found in that marriage. You need to discuss questions such as these regularly: "Are we willing to settle for what our marriage is becoming?" "Is our relationship mutually beneficial?" "Does our relationship embrace our uniqueness?"

Do you remember what it was like when your beloved told you, for the very first time, that he or she loved you? One woman shared her recollection with us. "How blue his eyes were and how warm," she said. "He smiled a beautiful smile at me and said, 'I've been waiting all my life for you.' " Even now, forty years later, the memory caused her eyes to moisten. She explained how her family were intellectual and well-mannered, but reserved people, who didn't believe in open demonstrations of affection. "When I looked into his eyes I felt great

notes

love and acceptance," she said. "For the first time in my adult life, I felt a deep sense of being welcomed, of mattering to someone."

DECISION THREE

"I Will Make Our Relationship a Priority"

A young couple sat in front of us. Tears tumbled down the wife's cheeks as she raised the option of separation. Her husband watched her with cold disdain. Arrogantly, he patted himself on the back for his commitment to the marriage. "I signed up to be husband, and that's what I am and will be, a husband," he said. "What more do you want?"

Her tears increased. She choked out these words: "I was under the misconception that part of the definition of husband was lover. We stopped being friends as soon as the wedding ceremony was over. The focused attention, the time spent talking, the dates and the kind words all stopped. You've wanted me to perform when you demanded it. You expected dinner, sex, and your clean clothes, but you withdrew into a shell, and I haven't been able to reach you since. It's as if you got me now, so you have to find a new challenge. I have no question that you're in this for life. After all, you're a man of your word. The question is, what kind of a life is this going to be?"

At that point her husband accused her of not being a committed Christian because she wasn't content in the marriage.

Do you think maybe he missed the point? Obviously, he did not get the Life Mate Poster Boy of the Year award.

As we discussed in chapter 1, commitment is the first principle of a satisfying marriage relationship, the critical decision that makes all other decisions possible. But if this foundational decision—the decision to lock the escape hatch and throw away the key—is the only decision you make in your marriage, then your spouse will feel that marriage is more of a life sentence than a life adventure. Commitment can be deliberate and decisive, or it can be simply dutiful. You and your spouse can embrace excellence or you can just endure.

What a difference it makes when we are motivated by love and not duty. It's the difference between staying in marriage because God hates divorce or viewing each day as an opportunity to really love each other as Christ loved us. We acknowledge with the Apostle John that if we don't love the person we can see, our spouse, how can we possibly love the God we can't see (1 John 4:20)?

Being "Us" on Purpose

When a couple arrives at our office for marriage counseling, we explain in the first session that even though both the husband and wife are tremendously important as individuals, we view the "client" to be their marriage relationship. Because of this perspective, there may be times that we have to challenge one or both of them to reconsider whether their actions or words build up or tear down the marriage. We make it clear that we don't keep secrets. If one person tells us something that the spouse doesn't know, we ask them to inform the other by the end of the next session or we will need to refer them to another therapist.

We choose to approach marital counseling this way because we see a couple's marriage as a separate entity, created by both of them and yet separate from either of them. This entity we refer to as a couple's "us." Each couple births a marriage relationship, an "us," just as they birth a newborn child. Can we stress that both births require intensive labor? Unfortunately, in some marriages, the "us" in reality is a "me." One spouse determines the type of marriage the couple has. Only one person's voice is heard.

Joan sets the pace in their relationship. Her husband, Don, is a quiet, easygoing sort of guy. He travels one week out of every month. When he is at home, his schedule is determined by her expectations. She sets the social agenda. She has an enormous honey-do list for him to complete. She decides when and if they have any sex. If he raises an issue that upsets her, she turns it back on him and makes him sorry he even approached the topic. She handles all the finances and regularly makes unilateral decisions in spite of his request for the contrary. She complains that he doesn't spend enough time with the children, but when he tries, she undermines his efforts. If you were to ask Joan about their "us," she would say that it is alive and well. What she doesn't see is that their so-called "us" is all about her and her agenda.

Across town, Bill makes sure that his wife's input falls on deaf ears. Over the years, Anne has attempted to raise her concerns over Bill's parenting style, his short fuse, and his absence of affection. He has disregarded her thoughts and feelings and condemned her for being nonsubmissive. She is tired of trying to get him to take her seriously. All of her emotional energy goes into her children. Bill thinks their "us" is thriving. Anne knows better. Their marriage is all about Bill.

Neither Joan and Don or Bill and Anne have created an "us." In their worlds, it is all about one of them. For both of these couples, "us" is really a "me."

In contrast, relationships that are loving, trustworthy, and growing welcome input from both partners. This couple's "us" takes on a personality that is a combination of the two of them. It is something unique and greater than either of them alone.

One husband gave this clear description of the "us" at work in their relationship. "I don't like ballet, but our 'us' does. When I say this, I do not mean that I just give in to my wife because she likes it, and I suffer through the performance. I mean that when I go with my wife, the activity becomes enjoyable, because of how we dress up to go, where we go to eat, and how we interact about the performance. Our relationship really does like the activity of ballet, even though I would never go by myself."[1]

Instead of asking how a father parents or how a mother parents, a couple needs to come to a place of agreement about how their "us" will best parent. Similarly, how does their "us" handle finances? What hobbies does their "us" share? Every "us" is unique to the couple creating it, just as each newborn is unique.

If either of you were to die, the one left would definitely grieve the loss of the other, but you would have more to grieve than that. You would have to grieve the loss of what you were together—your "us." What a loss that would be!

"Us" by Accident

Our "us" thrives as a newborn thrives when nurtured, given attention, cared for, and supported. Only neglectful parents would dream of abandoning their child after birth, but too often we treat our marriage that way after our honeymoon.

Because our "us" is invisible, it's easy to neglect or ignore it. We've heard the following words so many times:

> "I miss us. I miss how we used to sit, talk, laugh, and touch. The noise of the kids is exhausting, but the silence of our marriage screams."
>
> "I don't know what to talk about anymore."
>
> "I want you."
>
> "I want shared memories."

"I'm getting to the place where I feel nothing."

"I'm so tired."

"The rare times our eyes actually meet,
I'm looking into the eyes of a stranger."

"I'm so lonely."

"It's as if we all love our way to wholeness."

Couples who can declare these statements have a disconnect so great that they are like two singles living under the same roof—emotionally divorced although still married. It's as if their "us" has been shot and the gun is still smoking. While they may be faithful with their bodies, honoring part of their marriage vow by not having an affair, they are unfaithful with their hearts. They no longer love, honor, and cherish each other. Their marriage has no heart.

This is not what God intended. The word "woman" in Hebrew is a complementary word to "man." It hints at the idea that Adam and Eve together formed an even larger whole. Adam recognized Eve as his true counterpart.

In marriage, we cleave to each other. We are "glued" together, as it were. Ask anyone who is married: this doesn't happen instantaneously just because there has been a wedding ceremony. It is progressive. It happens day-by-day, month-by-month, and year-by-year. The "us" that is created in the process is not just about two separate individuals who both contribute to the relationship. It is also about a man and a woman who give up a part of themselves to create oneness, an "us."

What about your relationship? How would you describe it? Is it a legal obligation with absolutely no emotional connection? Is it primarily a relationship of fighting and discontent? Is it a bad decision, a temporary bump on your road to find the "perfect" mate? Is your "us" really a "me" created by only one person? Or is it an "us" that can promote individual and relational growth, that can handle conflict and that can deal with the complexities of each partner's perspective?

Choice: To grow or outgrow our "us."

Marriage on Purpose

A great Italian psychiatrist, Roberto Assagioli, wrote a parable about three fourteenth-century stonecutters who were working on a large cathedral. When the first stonecutter was asked what he was doing, he replied that he was cutting stones into blocks. When the second stonecutter was asked the same question, he said that he was earning a living for his beloved family. The third cutter's reply stopped the interviewer cold. In a joyous voice he told of the privilege of participating in the construction of a great cathedral that would stand as a holy lighthouse for thousands of years. The same menial task . . . but three different meanings assigned to it by three different men.

In Ephesians 5:15, Paul challenges each of us to live life with a due sense of responsibility, not as men who do not know the meaning and purpose of life, but as those who do. Why does your "us" exist? What difference is it going to make to the two of you and to your world that you are married?

Many of you may have created a personal or a business mission statement that clearly defines your purpose. Have you ever considered writing out a mission statement for your marriage? Each of us needs to be married on purpose. We asked a few couples to share their mission statement. Their responses were thought provoking.

> To magnify God together.
> To wisely develop and use our time, talents, and resources to help others.
> To build healthy, loving relationships in which we help each other become our best selves.

To be God's hands, arms, eyes, mouth, and feet to each other and then to the people in our circle of influence.
To have fun.
To be partners who love, cherish, honor, and enjoy each other.
To be parents our children come to for love, comfort, and understanding. To be faithful in the tasks and relationships that come across our path.
We exist to love consistently, to learn continually, to live courageously, and to leave a legacy with God's principles as our guide.

What is the purpose of your "us"? This may be a new thought for some of you. We would like to challenge you to do some brainstorming as a couple. In one or two sentences, try to summarize your marriage's purpose. Don't expect to complete this exercise quickly. It may take you a few weeks to refine your mission statement.

notes

A Calendar with Purpose

Not only is it valuable to create a marriage on purpose, we believe that it is

BOY, WHAT A CROWD. ARE YOU SURE WE NEED THIS?

crucial to visualize your mission statement on a daily basis. It is important to question whether or not the activities in your day move you toward your purpose.

Once you've established your purpose, it's important to think about your priorities. If building your "us" is a priority, you need "alone time together." Personally, we find it valuable to plan this on our weekly calendar. For those of you who groan at the mere thought of a schedule, preferring to let things happen spontaneously, we'd like to share a story told by one of Steve Covey's associates in the book *First Things First.*

An instructor was lecturing on time management. At one point he gave a quiz. He put a wide-mouth gallon jar and a platter offist-sized rocks on a table, and asked the participants how many rocks would fit into the jar.

Everyone made a guess, and then the instructor filled the jar with fist-sized rocks. Then he asked if it was full. The participants all agreed that indeed it was.

He reached under the table, pulled out a bucket of gravel, and dumped it into the jar. Then he shook the jar. Everyone watched as the gravel filled the spaces around the rocks. Again he asked, "Is the jar full?"

This time the participants said, "Probably not." The instructor picked up a bucket of sand and filled the jar to the brim. Again he asked the same question, "Is the jar full?"

The participants replied negatively. Then he poured a pitcher of water into the jar and asked, "What is the point of this illustration?"

One participant asked if he was trying to demonstrate that they could always squeeze more into their lives. The instructor said, "No, the point is this: If you hadn't put those big rocks in first, you would never have gotten any of them in." [2]

If you want to make your "us" a priority, then you have to schedule childless-couple time on your calendars. It is too easy to let the mundane and urgent tasks that need to be done crowd out your couple time.

Jan remembers: We learned the importance of this principle as a result of personal failure. When Dave was taking his doctorate, he was also working forty hours a week. We had very little time for each other. There would be an exam on Friday morning, and that would get his undivided attention when he was finally at home.

Around Thursday evening, I would be bent out of shape. Dave hadn't given our son or me virtually any time or attention all week. Instead of demonstrating a temporary moment of maturity, I'd demonstrate just the opposite. I'd lay the guilt on hard by saying, "Don't you care about Christopher and me?"

Often that would get Dave out of his books, but it was less than satisfying. I knew he was in the same room because I'd laid a guilt trip on him, but he was only halfheartedly there because he was still preoccupied. His mind was on his exam.

After much frustration, we decided to adopt a habit that radically affected our relationship. On Sunday evening, we sat down with an empty master calendar of the week. We discussed our priorities and put them on the calendar first. Couple time got top billing. Listed below are some of our priorities; don't think that you have to have the same entries on your calendar.

- A date time. Together brainstorm a list of possible activities you would enjoy sharing on a date night. Then we like to alternate responsibility for the planning.
- A daily connection time. Set aside 20 minutes a day to share a cup of coffee and to discuss the interesting things that happened in your day. This is a time to relax and "touch one another's heart" without necessarily "touching one another's parts."
- A time for sexual intimacy. If it happens more than once,

great! It's a super week. This way it at least happens once. If you choose to make love in the evening, perhaps the husband can put the kids to bed while giving his wife the gift of an hour alone to unwind.

- A weekly issue discussion time. Two thirty-to-sixty-minute slots to discuss the tough issues. We each get one time slot a week. That way our problems aren't discussed every day, all day, polluting an entire week.
- Daily prayer time together. Be intentional. When we pray for each other and show concern for each other's spiritual growth, we are demonstrating love in a powerful way.
- Personal and family weekly commitments. These are the events and activities that normally fill a week. Reviewing them together helps to prioritize and understand what the week may hold.

We can't emphasize enough what a major difference this has made in our relationship. We both feel as if we are living from the inside out. We are living on purpose. We are married on purpose. This way our "us" thrives even when we are busy.

If we believe that love and sexuality deserve time and attention, then we need to create a calendar that fits our priorities and purpose. It won't happen without the two of us deciding that it is important to both of us.

Having stressed how crucial it is to schedule couple time, now we would like to issue a warning: Seize the moment!

So often we put off something that would bring us joy because we didn't include it on our schedule, we didn't anticipate it, or we were too rigid to depart from routine.

We are like the little girl who spent all of her Christmas holidays behind the closed doors of her bedroom. Her single dad didn't know what to do. His wife had died of cancer three months before. Should he leave his little daughter alone? He kept inviting her to spend time with him.

On Christmas morning, to his surprise, she had a package under the tree for her daddy. When he opened it up, he discovered a pair of hand-knit socks. She said, "Daddy, I made these all by myself. That is what I was doing every day in my room."

With tears streaming down his cheeks, he held his precious daughter. "Honey, thanks for the beautiful socks, but all I really wanted was time with you."

When your husband or wife calls to surprise you with a spur-of-the-moment lunch, what is your response? "I can't." "I've got too much to do." "It's Monday."

Wrong answer. Let's try another: "Wow, what a surprise, I'll make it happen." Who knows what serendipities are in store for the two of you!

Make a special effort to touch each other as much as possible. Touch when you walk in and out of a room. Pat your spouse when you pass each other. Touch each other while eating dinner or watching the news. Rub his shoulders. Hold her hand. Kiss each other. Stroke his hair. Rub her back or feet every day. Make sure you are touching when you say you love each other or before you say good-night.

Dave notes: Sexual touching can be an exciting part of this, but don't make it the focus. Husbands, after being married thirty years, and counseling for twenty-five, I have discovered one principle: Touch your wife's heart before you touch her parts . . . the ones different from yours.

Most of us fell in love through rituals of intimacy. We maintain love in the same way. Refuse to have an ordinary marriage, a mediocre one. Move towards developing an "us" that thrills your soul.

Boundaries

If you are going to have a marriage on purpose, your "us" has to decide how it is going to guard against possible intruders into your marriage. It is possible for parents, children, work, leisure activities, ministry opportunities, addictions, and other people to be intruders into your relationship. Those who value their marriage will pay a high price to protect it.

Parents as Intruders

When we spoke our wedding vows, we both stepped out of our family circles and before God, our families, and friends, we created a new family circle distinct and separate from our parents and friends.

In the original creation, God made male and female to be together. Because of this, a man leaves father and mother, and in marriage he becomes one flesh "because God created this organic union of the two sexes, no one should desecrate his art by cutting them apart" (Mark 10:6-9, *The Message*).

The theme of leaving parents to become joined to one's spouse is the first reference to marriage in the Bible and is repeated five times. Leaving is more than geographical: it involves breaking dependence on parents and establishing a clear boundary with them. One's spouse now takes priority over one's parents. The Jews have a saying, "When a young man gets married, he divorces his mother."

Ideally, a couple is able to maintain a deep attachment with their parents without letting them intrude into their circle. This will only happen if a couple clarifies the boundary of their marriage relationship and the parents learn to honor that boundary. Incredible pain is caused when one spouse continues to allow or to foster parental intrusion in the marriage.

Dave and Sally were in trouble because Dave couldn't disappoint his mother. She was a widow, and he was a sensitive, caring son. Mother would phone and say she was coming for a three-month visit. Without so much as discussing this with his wife, he would tell his mom she was welcome. When his wife reacted because she hadn't been included in his unilateral decision, he accused her of selfishness. Sally felt misunderstood and angry because he had not protected the boundary of their marriage. Keeping Mother happy was more important to him than honoring their relationship.

Scripture is very clear that the marriage takes priority over the parental relationship. If your parents haven't retired from their parenting, you are going to have to fire them. Why? Because God designed parenting as a temporary job description. Parenting is the only relationship whose ultimate goal is to release a child to be his or her own person. Parenting is for a season. Once children are adults, further parenting will only be seen and felt as intrusion. What you now need from your parents is for them to become adult friends.

Children as Intruders

Parenthood is the state of being better chaperoned than you ever were before you got married. Children are demanding, needy, and time-eaters.

Jan: Dave and I are deeply committed to our children. We believe parenting is an incredibly important calling, but there were times we were out of balance. We overscheduled activities for our children, and underscheduled time and activities as a couple.

That is wrong, psychologically as well as spiritually. Carl Jung, the psychiatrist, said, "Nothing has a stronger influence on children than the unlived life of their parents." Every couple needs "childless times" on a weekly basis. We have to take care of our "us," so it can take care of our children.

The bedroom door needs to have hinges and a lock—hinges to

welcome the children, but also a lock to keep them out. The kids need to see that Mom and Dad have something separate and special that doesn't include them. This gives them a sense of safety and security.

A lot of us didn't get enough from our parents growing up, so we want to do the opposite. We don't ever want our children to feel abandoned, so we give in to their every desire. We feel we shouldn't ever leave them with a baby-sitter. If they want to sleep with us they should be able to. We shouldn't ever say no to them—in fact, that feels like we're being abusive.

We have confused limits with abuse. We have produced a generation of kids who know they are deeply loved, but are confused about their place in their family and the world. They expect to be primary. They expect us to cater to them.

Ron brought twin thirteen-year-old boys into his new marriage with Ginger. In the previous family, the kids had ruled the roost. There were few rules and little supervision. Ron and Ginger attended parenting classes before they got married and decided to do some things differently. The boys were in shock, and all their resentment was directed at Ginger.

Ron wanted to honor the boundary around his new marriage. He sat down with his teenagers. He validated their feelings, empathized with them, but then apologized to them. "It is not your new mom, it's me," he said. "I did this to you. My passivity and lack of follow-through while you were growing up was destructive to you. I don't want to make this mistake again. I will always listen to you, but there are certain values that we follow in this home."

Ginger felt supported and protected by her husband. He hadn't allowed his children to drive a wedge between them. Her husband's words and actions kept her from being labeled as the wicked stepmother.

Work, Leisure Activities, Ministry Opportunities

When we can't say no to anything, our hearts get removed from each other. Being busy can be an anesthetic to the emptiness of a marriage. Each of us needs to evaluate ourselves on a regular basis.

Addictions

If your spouse is abusing alcohol or using drugs, you know what it is like to try to establish a relationship with someone who is unavailable. The bottom line is, you can't! It is an impossible task because your spouse is having an affair with a substance, and you are excluded.

Shopping or gambling taken to the extreme can put tremendous pressure on a marriage and bring a couple to bankruptcy. Husbands and wives can both struggle with this. Each of us needs to set appropriate boundaries on ourselves and on our desires.

If your spouse happens to be addicted to pornography, not only will this have a devastating impact on you, but it will also leave you feeling ashamed, doubting yourself, doubting your sexual attractiveness, feeling rejected and abandoned. The Bible is extremely clear about maintaining the boundary around a couple's sexual relationship. "Honor marriage, and guard the sacredness of sexual intimacy between wife and husband. God draws a firm line against casual and illicit sex" (Hebrews 13:4, *The Message*).

Friends and Supporters

A six-year-old boy was asked how he could tell if people were married. His reply: "Married people look happy to talk to others."

Ouch! There have been times in our relationship when we had more fun with friends than we did with each other. We had to face that fact, cut back on our activities with friends, and concentrate on bringing that fun back into our marriage. This is yet another example of the good robbing the best.

Joan's husband, Jim, was everybody's friend. If anyone, including his ex-wife, needed some help, a favor, or a shoulder to cry on, they would call on Jim, who would drop whatever he was doing and immediately run to his or her side. One day, Joan approached Jim. What saddened her was that it appeared to her that Jim was everyone else's friend but not hers. Her expression of need was often ignored as he went off to assist someone else.

Jim listened long and hard and took her words seriously. A few days later, Jim got a phone call from his ex-wife. She had another project that she needed his help with. "I'm sorry, but I'm behind on my marriage," said Jim. "I haven't spent enough time with Joan. I need to make her top priority. She needs me this evening. Here is the phone number of someone who could assist you."

Can you imagine how loved Joan felt?

It is our belief that every married couple needs people who support their lifelong commitment to each other. It takes others in the body of Christ to support us, challenge us, and pray for us. That helps each of us return to our marriage feeling energized.

Warning: Without the boundary of marriage being honored, the request for prayer can easily turn into gossip.

If Gail is married to Gordon and he hurts Gail, instead of telling Gordon that she is hurt, Gail can rush off to tell Sally, her prayer partner, how Gordon needs prayer. The first thing Sally needs to do is to send Gail back to communicate with her husband. Sally needs to support the marriage—the couple, not just the spouse who is complaining at that point in time. Sally can commit to pray for Gail as she goes back to talk with Gordon.

What if Gail, instead of going to Sally, reaches out to one of the men at work who just happens to have been sharing his marriage woes with her? He tells Gail his wife doesn't have time for him, doesn't listen to him, and takes him for granted. He says that she never finished college and isn't as intelligent as Gail. In fact, he says all his wife can talk about is the kids. Last Wednesday, he told Gail how beautiful she was. Gail is headed for disaster if she chooses to take her pain and discuss it with someone of the opposite sex. She has put herself in a very vulnerable place.

We have sat in counseling with many shocked people who never dreamed that they were capable of having an affair. We all are capable of stumbling. We can't forget our humanity. We need to guard the boundaries of our marriages.

Your complaints need to be brought to your husband or wife to be discussed. If that leads to deadlock, then it is crucial that the two of you together seek an unbiased third party, a pastor, a counselor, or a trusted couple. Whomever you choose as your confidante needs to be committed to your marriage rather than taking sides.

Jan: Warning: It is important to bring your fantasy life into your marriage. Dave and I have covenanted to tell one another when we are attracted to someone else or someone expresses an attraction to us. At that time, we sit down and ask, "What does this mean? Are there unmet needs in our marriage? Have we been crabby lately? Are there some things we need to talk about? Is there something we need to change in how we relate to each other?" We have found in our counseling that what is talked about is less likely to be acted out! What is put into words is usually not put into action!

The reality is, in one way or another, in the past most of us have been guilty of allowing one of these intruders—parents, kids, other people, work, ministry, leisure activities, and addictions—into our marriage relationship. Our purpose is not to condemn you, judge you, put you down, or dredge up your past. Rather, we want to challenge you to look ahead and make different choices to protect the boundary of your marriage. It doesn't matter half as much where you've been as where your "us" is headed.

There is no question that tough times will come, and tension will rear its head. Your spouse will irritate you (you read it here), you'll press each other's buttons, and you'll surprise and sometimes disappoint each other. There will be times that you will have to put intruders in their place. Through it all if you have, on a daily basis, made your "us" important and your relationship a priority, you'll be motivated to do the necessary work when you get out of sync because you know how good the good can be.

I want us to be more
than just "an old married couple."
I want us to be silly and romantic
And even irresponsible from time to time!
I want us to flirt and always keep on
Trying to be our best for each other,
Like we did when we first met.
I know we both have days
When we're tired—
That's only human.
But I just don't want
Us to ever take each other for granted.
I want to always keep the fire
between us smoldering.
I want us to be able to
Share everything
And to make our love
a source of strength in our lives.
And from now on,
I'm going to do all I can
To always make time for us,
Because I consider
our "love affair" to be a lifetime thing.
- Anonymous

Decision #3
"I Will Make Our Relationship a Priority"

For Reflection and Discussion

1. Have your children evaluate your intimacy (if you dare!) by scoring you in the following manner:

   1—Disagree

   2—Somewhat Disagree

   3—Somewhat Agree

   4—Agree

   ____ Mom and Dad speak highly of each other, even when the other one isn't there.

   ____ Mom and Dad hug and kiss in front of me.

   ____ Mom and Dad hold hands sometimes.

   ____ Mom and Dad talk to each other alone.

   ____ Mom and Dad surprise one another once in awhile.

   ____ Mom and Dad express their love for each other in front of us.

   ____ Mom and Dad touch each other.

   ____ Mom and Dad enjoy being together and it shows.

   ____ Mom and Dad don't put us in the middle of an argument.

   ____ Mom and Dad have interests they enjoy together.

   ____ When Mom and Dad argue, I'm sure they will work out their problem.

   ____ Mom and Dad regularly date each other.

   ____ When Mom and Dad's door is shut, we know not to interrupt.

   ____ Mom and Dad like each other.

   ____ Mom and Dad are honest with each other.

If your child rated you below 45, then you have some work to do! But it can be the most rewarding work in the world!

2. Commit to a time of weekly connection and evaluation. These are the kinds of questions you might consider discussing:

How did I do last week as a spouse to you?

Is there any way we are allowing our parents to intrude in our marriage?

Is our relationship with each other primary and our relationship with our kids secondary? Do we have a couple-centered or child-centered relationship?

Am I becoming a workaholic who has no time for my spouse?

Is my involvement at church or in the community leaving me with no time to spend with my mate?

Are my leisure activities (television, computers), sports, and hobbies robbing us of couple time?

Is our marriage relationship being destroyed by addictions? (If your answer is yes, we strongly suggest professional counsel.)

Am I investing more time and energy in my friendships than I am in my marriage?

When I've been hurt by my spouse, do I directly communicate my hurt to my spouse or do I run off to tell someone else?

Do the supportive people in my life support my marriage as well as me? Do they help me see the good in my spouse?

DECISION FOUR

"I Will Revisit My Expectations"

Linda found herself increasingly depressed. Wasn't marriage supposed to make her happy? What a crock. She was miserable. She felt betrayed by her young husband, Tom, and let down by marriage in general.

Linda had always loved Tom's strength and compassion. She had spent hours dreaming about the times of Bible study and prayer—the spiritual connection they would share together. Her dreams were dashed. Tom rarely, if ever, opened his Bible. He didn't have time to. When he was at home he was glued to the TV watching sporting events. Prior to marriage she'd enjoyed sports with him, but she had no idea that he spent every waking hour of his weekend watching TV.

She'd assumed that he would want to spend Christmas at her parents' house, but he let her know that he had no such intention. He wanted them to go on a ski trip together. Mom and Dad would be furious if they knew, especially after the fortune they had spent on the wedding.

When they were dating, Tom always seemed so thoughtful and considerate. Now he seemed quite comfortable letting her take the lion's share of the home responsibilities. In addition, it felt to her as if every time he touched her he wanted to go to bed. She wanted just to snuggle, but that seemed to be the impossible dream. She found herself thinking, Why did I get married? It was better at Mom and Dad's.

Tom was having his own challenges. He had assumed that Linda, who was a Christian when he married her, would want to stay at home taking care of his every need. She not only wanted to work, but she wanted to go back to school part-time. He discovered that she wasn't as frugal as he had believed. Sometimes she didn't plan ahead very well. She hadn't gotten the grocery shopping done the other day, which meant she had to do it after work. It was nine o'clock before he had any dinner. After dinner, she rebuffed his advances. Was this the same woman who couldn't keep her hands off him when they were dating? This wasn't what he'd imagined when he got married.

> We love because it is the only true adventure.

Tom and Linda held unconscious, uncommunicated, unrealistic, and unreasonable expectations. As a result, each felt betrayed, as if the other had broken a promise. Yet no promise had ever been made. They had many expectations of each other, but had not shared them or agreed on them.

Mary Lou and Jason entered their marriage with a sense of doom and gloom. They weren't sure that they could make it. Twenty-two years later, they still weren't sure. It was if they'd been driving through marriage with their brakes on the entire way.

Mary Lou's version of her best friends' marriages was that each of these couples were just existing. "Two of them got married when they were young. Twenty years later it seems as if they have outgrown each other. One of them has never recovered from her husband's affair. Two friends aren't even sleeping in the same bedroom with their husbands anymore. Their kids know that they are miserable."

Jason also had been deeply affected by the grim statistics on marriage, so much so that his fear has distorted how he looked at his own marriage. In his mind he had turned differences into problems, and these problems appeared irreconcilable.

Any idealism about marriage he'd ever had was dashed by the way they argued. In the midst of an angry exchange, they'd both said some terrible things that they'd never meant to say. They had even threatened divorce. They'd both apologized, expressed their sorrow, and recommitted to the marriage, but Jason was afraid of history repeating itself. He vowed never to go there again. He distanced from Mary Lou in order to feel some sense of safety.

Mary Lou had sensed Jason's withdrawal and had pulled away herself. When she'd think of things that Jason might enjoy, she'd talk herself out of them. Why bother, why should she be the one to make the first move? She was bored, depressed, and lonely. It was as if she didn't even know who Jason was anymore. Did he even care about her?

Both Mary Lou and Jason enjoyed movies. Lately, it seemed to them that infidelity was rather routine. Every newspaper or magazine had a report of some celebrity marriage's rift and rupture. Was it possible for anyone to be happily married any more?

Two couples, at different life stages, find themselves battling their expectations and, as a result, battling each other.

Confusion Runs Rampant

Each of us enters marriage with preconceived notions of how things should be. The belief that we are entitled to personal happiness has become the central imperative in many of our lives. Happiness has become more important than family. Human beings are sacrificed regularly to this end. We believe in love, but we also believe in self. This belief has resulted in ambivalence about marriage and its possibilities.

As a culture, we have so idealized marriage that we have turned it into the primary vehicle for personal, emotional, and spiritual transformations. According to an internationally known market research company, Iconoculture, a longtime first marriage—twenty-five years or more—has become a status symbol in corporate America.[1] Our society has fallen in love with the idea of being loved. We insinuate that we can be "soul mates." A love relationship is where we're supposed to feel most at home.

Ralph put it this way, "I feel so much support from Joyce. She is always there for me. No one has ever cared for me like this." Pauline glowed as she put her thoughts into words by saying, "I feel at home with Peter. I now feel like I belong in the world. I love being the recipient of his love and attention."

On the other hand, we find ourselves so demoralized by marriage that we discard the institution easily when it no longer gratifies us. It's as if divorce has become a new stage in the quest for the ideal relationship. We marry, divorce, and remarry in hopes of ending up in a happy marriage. According to Barbara Defoe Whitehead, most remarriages happen within three years following a divorce. Judith Wallerstein, in her latest book, *The Unexpected Legacy of Divorce: A 25-Year Landmark Study*, states that adult children of divorce, while believing in the institution of marriage, expect to fail at marriage. They fear loss, conflict, betrayal, and loneliness.[2]

Our media, through movies, TV, and romance novels, promote the themes of sex, passion, and romance. Often these stories are of unmarried couples or married partners who are having affairs. The story, like a fairytale, usually ends when the couple falls in love, and with stars in their eyes starts life together.

At the same time that we have maximized our expectations for emotional fulfillment in marriage, we, as a culture, have minimized our sense of obligation and commitment to the institution of marriage. The same media that raised our expectations for marriage now seem to consider "failure to thrive" as the status quo for most marriages. When babies fail to thrive, it is considered a disaster and an emergency—not so with marriage. In addition, there is the self-help market that leads us to believe that we can get anything we want from marriage if we only learn the right skills.

When marriage doesn't live up to its advertisement, as it can't, the same media deliver it a death sentence. It is considered obsolete, a life sentence,and a trap. How could one person possibly meet all of our needs over a lifetime? Perhaps it is a relevant institution if you are going to have children, but who really knows? Children are resilient.

Humorists have a heyday with the topic of marriage:

"Matrimony isn't a word, it's a sentence."

"Marriage is usually due to lack of judgment, divorce to lack of patience, and remarriage to lack of memory."

"Insanity is grounds for divorce in some states, but grounds for marriage in others."

Is it any wonder that we find ourselves confused?

Revisit Expectations

We often see what life has made us ready to see. Frankly, our own selfish desires and our media have set us up to see marriage as both our salvation and our greatest disappointment. Mistaking our perceptions for reality is one of the root causes of suffering. Perceptions can bring a sense of hope and order to our world, but often at the expense of limiting our experience of life. This is especially true when our perceptions are based on illusions. As Garrison Keillor wrote, "Sometimes you have to look reality in the eye and deny it."[3]

The good news is that our expectations are within our control! Healthy couples identify and examine their expectations whenever they feel disappointment or a sense of betrayal. They ask themselves questions like "What did I expect that I didn't get?" and "Is it wise to expect this or do I need to change my expectation?"

The Memphis public school system has a legend brought to light by Bill O'Hanlon. One year there was a class of students who were so unruly, they burned out two different teachers. One teacher took an early retirement, and the other decided to get out of teaching altogether. This class was so bad that substitute teachers refused to take it, so the district called a teacher who had applied for a job, but hadn't made the cut that year. They asked her if she would be willing to come in and finish out the year in return for the promise of a full-time position the next year. She eagerly accepted. The principal decided not to warn the teacher about the class, afraid that she would be scared off if she knew what she was up against.

notes

After the teacher had been on the job for one month, the principal sat in on the class to see how things were going. To his amazement, the students were well behaved and enthusiastic. After the students filed out of the class, the principal stayed around to congratulate the teacher on a job well done. The teacher thanked him.

"You see, I discovered your little secret on my first day here," she said. "I looked in the desk drawer and found the list of the students' IQ scores. I knew I had a challenging group of kids here, so bright and rambunctious that I would really have to work to make school interesting for them because they were so intelligent." She slid the drawer open, and the principal saw the list of the students names and the numbers 136, 145, 127, 128, and so on written next to their names. It turns out she was reading their locker numbers.[4]

What kind of expectations do you hold about your marriage? When our perceptions about love, about marriage, about ourselves and about our mate are colored by immature, unrealistic, and unreasonable expectations, we can't see beyond the veil of our own judgments and demands. Our beliefs keep us from seeing reality. The Talmud puts it well, "We do not see things as they are, we see things as we are." Yet often we try to make our lives and our marriages conform to the unreality of our expectations.

Removing the Rose-colored Lens . . .
. . . About Marriage

Over the years in our counseling offices, we have seen tremendous pain caused by unreasonable expectations of marriage. Couples seem to fluctuate between believing that marriage has failed them and that they have failed marriage. Have you felt disillusionment in your own relationship as a result of believing any of these myths?:

A good marriage is problem free.

A good marriage makes all our dreams come true.

A good marriage will solve all our problems.

A good marriage involves no pain.

A good marriage always has high romance and passion.

A good marriage can make up for a lousy childhood.

A good marriage will rescue us from our own unhappiness and loneliness

A good marriage is 50/50.

A marriage is good only if it feels good.

There is one perfect way to do marriage.

It's as if we view marriage as a beautiful box full of everything we've always wanted and never quite gotten in relationship. We seem to believe that all we have to do is reach into that box and pull out intimate communication, spirituality, passionate romance, great sex, fun, companionship, and total acceptance. This box is going to ensure that we feel no more pain or loneliness or doubt.

Eventually we have to face the truth. At the beginning of our marriage, our box is empty. There will be nothing in our marriage box that we haven't put into it.

- There is no love in marriage. There is love in people, who can then choose to put love into their marriage box.
- There is no adventure in marriage. But there are adventuresome people who may choose to bring that aspect of themselves into their relationship.
- There is no romance in marriage. If romance is something that both partners value, they will build it into their marriage.

Periodically, every couple needs to stop and examine what they've been putting into their marriage box.

. . . About Love

Our culture, through music, books, magazines, movies, and TV, has idealized the love bond. At the beginning of a relationship it's almost as if the couple worships each other. She talks excitedly with her friends about finding the "love of her life." He talks about the "woman of his dreams." Together they believe that love will conquer all. There will be no conflict, heartache, or misunderstanding. They can't imagine that these loving feelings could ever fluctuate and in fact, if they do, the couple assumes that they are no longer in love.

What is wrong with these beliefs? They sound so plausible. "Love is patient, love is kind. It does not envy, it does not boast, it is not proud. It is not rude, it is not self-seeking, it is not easily angered, it keeps no record of wrongs. Love does not delight in evil but rejoices with the truth. It always protects, always trusts, always hopes, always perseveres" (1 Corinthians 13:4-7).

Love is an action. It is something we do. To assume that love is a feeling is to confuse it with attraction and infatuation. It is by habitually depositing acts of kindness and consideration into our marital box that love becomes a reality.

. . . About Our Partners

Ideal relationships set us up. Real relationships turn us on. Many heartaches are caused by people who spend every waking moment pining for the mate of their dreams rather than appreciating the human being that they chose and who chose them.

Jan: Dave and I were no exception. We remember the night about three months into our marriage when we sat down with separate pieces of paper to write out what we expected from each other. We exchanged lists and laughed. Believe us, there was no place for imperfection! Only God Himself could have lived up to these expectations, but I don't think He would have been interested. They were so totally self-focused.

In a Yankelovich poll for Time/CNN, nearly eighty percent of men and women polled reported that they thought they would eventually find the perfect mate.[5] We still believe that somewhere out there that perfect person waits for us.

Did you go into marriage believing any of these statements?

If you love me, you'll be my "soul mate," making my life whole and complete.

If you love me, I will never have to verbalize my needs and desires.
If you love me, you will never criticize me.
If you love me, you'll see things the way I do.
If you love me, you'll never be attracted to anyone else.
If you love me, we'll never disagree.
If you love me, our differences won't matter.
If you love me, you won't need any other relationships.

Talk about the impossible dream! It's as if fantasy turns the person you're going to marry into someone without whom your life can't be sustained. Perhaps holding on to such unrealistic expectations led this woman to create the following letter, circulated on the Internet.

Dear Friend,

This letter was started by a woman in hopes of bringing relief to other tired and discontented women. Unlike most chain letters, this one does not cost anything.

Just bundle up your husband and send him to the woman whose name appears at the top of the list. Then add your name to the bottom of the list and send a copy of this letter to five of your friends who are equally tired and discontented. When your name comes to the top of the list, you will receive 3,325 men . . . and some of them are bound to be better than the one you gave up!

Do not break this chain! One woman did and she received her own husband back.

At this writing, a friend of mine had already received 184 men. They buried her yesterday, but it took four undertakers thirty-six hours to get the smile off her face.

Sincerely,

A disappointed woman

It seems that, in many marriages, when our unreasonable expectations aren't met by our partners, we turn on them and think seriously about discarding them. We must have made a mistake. We must have married the wrong person. We seem to neglect the reality that if our spouses could love us in all these ways, we'd never have the need to grow, stretch, or mature. We wouldn't have to assume any personal responsibility. We would always get things our way. We would lack empathy. We would be rigid and unbending. We would be selfish, arrogant, and egotistical.

Our unreasonable and unrealistic expectations betray our motivation. We want the world to rotate around us. Our partners exist in our fantasy world only to satisfy us. If they perform, our life will be pain free. James pinpoints our problem: "What causes fights and quarrels among you? Don't they come from your desires that battle in you (4:1)?"

Instead of divorcing our mates, perhaps it would serve us well to divorce these unreasonable and unrealistic expectations. As sports agent Leigh Steinberg said, "Never underestimate the capacity of another human being to have exactly the same shortcomings you have."

What is the truth about your spouse? He or she is human, which makes that person imperfect, immature, and different from you. What is the truth about you? You are human, and therefore imperfect, immature, and different from your husband or wife.

Reveal Your Expectations

So where do we go from here? First you must identify and question your expectations. Get honest with your partner. Clarify what your expectations are. Your husband or wife is not a mind reader and never will be.

Julie seemed impossible to please. When James kissed her, it always seemed to be an inappropriate time. When he'd watch their two little boys, it seemed that she spent most of her time watching him and waiting to find some flaw in his parenting style. When they were making love, she would lie there like a bump on a log as if daring him to excite her in any way. He was tired and discouraged. When he suggested that they sit down and write out their expectations for each other, at first she balked. She insinuated that if he really loved her, he would know what they were. He informed her that he couldn't read her mind, that he needed specifics. It took counsel from a therapist before James and Julie both came to see that identifying and communicating their expectations increased the possibility of getting their needs met. It also saved them a lot of grief.

We often find ourselves amazed, when we get specific with one another, that we could have spent so many years in close proximity without discovering such obvious differences of style and opinion. C'est la vie. Love may be blind, but marriage is a real eye-opener.

Release Unrealistic Expectations

Unrealistic expectations lead to disappointment. An elderly gentleman who had been married sixty years was asked the secret of his marriage. His reply was profound. "I guess back when we got married we didn't expect as much, and somehow we got more than we expected."

Carolyn relaxed in her marriage when she identified and questioned her expectations. She discovered that many of them were unreasonable and unrealistic. Like the house built on the sand, her fantasies about marriage had left her emotionally unstable.

She started by giving up her fantasy of "happily ever after." Did that mean she expected disaster? No, she expected marriage to be like life, predictable and unpredictable. There would be times of challenge and adversity as well as times of great celebration. It would require adjustment and readjustment on her part. Every other relationship she'd ever been a part of had had bumps and friction.

Why had she thought marriage would be any different?

She'd been married three years, long enough to know that Ron certainly wasn't perfect. She had to admit that even though that was disappointing, it also came as a great relief. She didn't do too well in the perfection department either.

In a moment of self-reflection she had to acknowledge that at the beginning of their marriage she'd made differences somehow bad. Differences weren't bad. They were just different. In fact, she'd been talking to an older couple at church. They described their forty-three year marriage as "happily incompatible."

That had made her think. Why did she emotionally withdraw when Ron's perspective was different from hers? What was that about? She'd never thought of herself as rigid, but was she? When Ron didn't support her viewpoint, questioned her bottom line or suggested alternatives, she found it challenging to welcome his perspective and rethink her position. Agreeing to disagree was difficult for her, yet she wanted their marriage to be big enough for both of them. She just had never expected them to see things so differently.

There were times that his differences were exhilarating. She loved to hear his deep, masculine laugh. She loved to snuggle into those strong arms, and the other day, he had helped her see a work challenge from a completely different perspective.

In the process of questioning whether her expectations were realistic or not, Carolyn thought back over the times she'd gotten angry with Ron in the last month. What she discovered surprised her. There was the time that she'd wanted him to do something the way her family had done it, and he questioned the wisdom of that. Another time she'd wanted him just to sense what she'd needed even though she hadn't communicated her desire to him. And then there was the decorating issue when she got angry because he wouldn't do it her way. Carolyn had to admit that often she simply expected too much from Ron. Happiness was her job, not his. She had to learn to take responsibility for getting her own needs met in ways that wouldn't threaten their relationship. She wanted to share his life, not run it.

It began to dawn on Carolyn that releasing her unrealistic expectations was a spiritual journey. The psalmist David's prayer became hers. "Search me, O God, and know my heart; test my thoughts. Point out anything you find in me that makes you sad" (Psalm 139:23, TLB).

Facing what marriage and her new husband brought her way helped to develop her character. When she stopped fighting reality, she found that her perspective of God, herself, and her husband, had shifted. Marriage required adulthood of her, and that meant that she had to face reality and release her unrealistic expectations. She was being transformed by love.

Resist Turning Expectations into Demands

Love can't be forced. It flows out of fullness, not fear. When we turn our expectations into demands, individuality is stifled, freedom is destroyed, and love is damaged. Jesus never forced Himself or His will on another person. We must resist forcing our partners to fit our expectations and projecting our values on them as if somehow ours are pure and theirs aren't. Our demands are not scriptural mandates. Conformity isn't the goal; understanding is.

Curt believes that as the husband he has the God-given right to demand that his wife meet his every expectation. His attitude is rigid and uncompromising. He is the conqueror, and she the conquered. He barks. She jumps. In his mind she owes him because he has given her a home, children, and financial support. In return, she should obey him without question. If she fails, he has the God-given right to punish her and to force compliance. As long as she never disagrees, they can spend a lifetime coexisting. The constant question in their home is "Who is in charge?" For her emotional and physical safety, her answer had better be, "You are, dear."

Domination is not headship. Demands are not love. Selfishness knows no gender lines. Any mate who approaches his or her partner with demands is acting out of selfishness and not love. Think about this: it was our mates' unique qualities that attracted us to them in the first place. How challenging it can be to accept that differing perspective when it is in conflict with the way we think the world should be.

When we are frustrated because our demands aren't being met, our feelings are temporarily so strong that we may feel justified in forcing the issue. With all the self-righteousness we can muster, we see the problem as "the other guy's" failure.

Sometimes, perhaps, we may even spiritualize the issue. We adopt the victim stance and believe that no one else has to deal with the burden we carry. We get others to feel sorry for us, and we remove our hearts from each other. We focus only on what our spouses aren't doing. We stop bringing anything loving to our marriages.

What effect does this have on our partners? If they have no choice but to meet our demands, then they become puppets. Love disappears when freedom is lost. Either they suck it up and meet our demands resentfully, or they imitate us and become equally negative, defensive, and demanding. It won't be long until we are deadlocked.

Jesus warns us: "Do not judge, or you too will be judged. For in the same way you judge others, you will be judged, and with the measure you use, it will be measured to you" (Matthew 7:1,2). When we feel justified in our demands and yet never question the expectations that are under the demands, freedom, joy, love, and growth are blocked in our relationships.

Renegotiate Your Expectations

Success in marriage doesn't come as the result of finding the right mate, but in the ability of both partners to adjust to the reality of the person they married. The more diverse your backgrounds, the more you will view life through different lenses. Expectations need to be discussed. It takes profound respect for your husband or wife and the value of your marriage to speak up and say, "I care enough about you and our relationship to raise the issues that are important to me."

Ryan sat down with his wife, Marsha. They had waited ten years to have children. Now that their precious baby had arrived, Marsha had lost all interest in sex. Ryan let her know that he loved their sexual relationship. He expressed his commitment to her and their little one, but he voiced his frustration at their lack of physical intimacy. He asked Marsha to respond to his request. After all, she was the only woman who could meet his need. Was she willing?

Reliable communication permits progress.

Marsha opened up to Ryan. She talked to him about her exhaustion. She let him know that she was feeling guilty for not being physically intimate with him and yet she was so tired. Not only did the baby want to be nursing all the time, but it felt as if Ryan wanted her body too. She went on to tell him that once they began cuddling, she found herself longing just to be cradled in the comfort of his arms without any expectation being put on her. She knew that he wanted more than that, and so her guilt would rear its head again.

They talked together into the wee hours of the morning. Marsha asked Ryan if they could schedule their lovemaking session for the next Saturday evening. Would he consider taking the baby for the afternoon so she could get some time off? How about Chinese takeout that evening for dinner? Would he hold her and giving her a back massage prior to their lovemaking?

Ryan felt that her requests were reasonable. He said he'd be happy to be on duty Saturday afternoon. Then he asked Marsha if she would agree to have sex at least once a week. Could they schedule it? Would she initiate it at least once a month? He didn't want to feel he was forcing her to do something she didn't want to do. Marsha understood. She wanted to know how she could tell him if their scheduled time wasn't going to work for her. Was there an acceptable way to say no? Ryan reassured her that there was, but that he then needed her commitment to reschedule. Could she give him that?

In a healthy marriage, we respond to each other's needs even if they are not the same as ours. Your husband or wife does not exist just for you. You must expect him or her to have a personal perspective, at times completely different from yours. This requires that you both adjust, just as Ryan and Marsha did.

Adjustment isn't natural, normal, or easy. Frankly, it takes character. It takes both self-restraint and humility. When we're rigid and unwilling to adjust, we drive away those closest to us. Solomon calls this choice foolish: "The fool who provokes his family to anger and resentment will finally have nothing worthwhile left" (Proverbs 11:29, TLB).

When you express an expectation, your partner can respond in one of three ways.

- "Sure I have absolutely no problem with that request. I didn't understand how important this was to you."
- "Thanks for telling me this. I can meet this at times. How can I let you know when I'm unable to meet your request?"
- "I'm sorry, but it's impossible for me to meet that expectation for these reasons."

Ideally we'd love to always hear the first response, but that isn't realistic. There are times that one person has no problem with the other's expectation, but does take issue with his or her version of that expectation.

Perhaps one of you is a neatnik, while the other one is far more relaxed about cleaning. There is a gap between what one expects and what the other is doing. Both partners will have to adjust. One hopes that, after hearing the neater partner's heart and realizing that there is no demand, the more relaxed partner can adjust the position and meet the other one partway. Perhaps the couple will agree that the public areas in their home will be picked up on a daily basis. They might decide that the door into the relaxed partner's office will always be shut. The organized chaos can thrive in that room.

Realistically, there are times in every marriage when both partners choose not to adjust their positions. What happens then? We can honestly express our disappointment. We can say that we hope that our mates will reexamine their position at some future time. Then we take our disappointment to God but refuse to nag, condemn, resent, or subject our mates to some other lack of grace. If our partners can never say no to us, then their yes is meaningless.

Give your spouse first chance to meet your needs. If he or she is unable or unwilling, then get the appropriate needs met by same-sex friends. Each of us needs to draw on the fellowship we find in the body of Christ. Your partner is incapable of meeting your every need.

If you are the one who has chosen not to meet your spouse's expectation for whatever reason, maturity is still required of you. You have to allow your mate to have feelings of disappointment and grief.

One of the most loving choices we can make to benefit our relationship is to revisit our expectations. In the process, we will learn how to recognize acts of love coming our way even if the delivery is different from what we expected. We will grow in our understanding of love and our appreciation of freedom. We will mature personally. God will be God, and we will be human lovers of each other. Love is a long series of choices made on a daily basis. Revisiting our expectations is an important choice.

Decision #4
"I Will Revisit My Expectations"

For Reflection and Discussion

1. How would you complete these sentences?

   A good wife is . . .

   A good husband is . . .

   A good marriage is . . .

2. What expectations do you have around these topics? Share your expectations with your spouse.

   Children
   Spirituality
   Chores
   My career
   Irritations
   Honesty
   Your career
   Together time
   Parents
   Finances
   Separate time
   Hobbies
   Sex
   Sleep time
   Problems
   Friends
   Decision making
   Emotional reactions

3. What are three unrealistic expectations that limit my growth and that get in the way of my contentment? What if I changed my expectation? Write a new belief in place of the previous unrealistic expectation.

4. If we both replaced our three unrealistic expectations with three new belief statements, how would our marriage be affected?

5. Ask yourself: Am I placing demands on my spouse? What am I doing to him or her as a result? What is our marriage becoming because of my demands? What must I do to improve our relationship?

DECISION FIVE

"I Will Champion You"

When we champion our spouses, we let them know they matter to us.

Have you ever experienced the wonder of having someone who championed you . . . believed in you, fought for you, encouraged you, and challenged you to see yourself through new eyes? When one is championed, it is like oxygen to the soul. It frees the spirit. It opens one up to grow, to learn, and yes, even to change.

When we sense that someone is "for" us, our loyalty toward that person deepens. When we hear words of affirmation, we are motivated. We feel new life and everything is right with the world. When we are championed, we are changed!

At the start of a new relationship, we tend to focus on the good. We overestimate the positive and put blinders on about the negative. But the closer we grow to one another, the more we become aware of areas we don't like, which leaves us uncomfortable. We begin to struggle with each other's imperfections. If we aren't intentional about championing right from the start, we can move from number one admirer to number one critic in one single marriage ceremony.

Mrs. Horowitz had a diamond the size of an egg. Her friend told her she was lucky to have such a fabulous jewel. Mrs. Horowitz replied, "Truly I am lucky, but along with the Horowitz diamond comes the Horowitz curse." "And what is that?" her friend inquired. Mrs. Horowitz replied, "Mr. Horowitz."

Are you tolerant of your partner? Unstable couples make an art form out of pointing out one another's limitations, faults, and weaknesses. It's quite easy to become invested in a negative view of your mate. Marriages don't just fall into a big black hole of dissatisfaction; rather, they begin as a relatively slow decline and pick up speed.

As children, we delighted in completing the little games that used to appear in coloring books under the caption, "What's wrong with this picture?" If you studied the picture carefully, you'd notice that the chair had only three legs and the clock was upside down. It was such fun to zero in on the mistakes. Unfortunately, some of us have never outgrown this game. We seem to derive our greatest satisfaction from focusing on what is missing, what is wrong, and what is broken. Everything and everyone around us fall short. We damage the spirit of those we love.

But once again there is good news: you are not at the mercy of your thoughts or feelings. Choose to focus on what you love about each other and your relationship instead of noticing only what fits your condemnation of your mate. Choosing to see your husband or wife from a new perspective can improve your view.

Nothing reinforces defensive behavior more than judgment, comparison, or rejection. One partner's critical spirit will make the other dig in his or her heels. After all, no one wants to be made over into a spouse's image. We want to grow up into God's image. We want to be our best selves.

Would those closest to you say that you spend more time voicing gratitude for and appreciation of your spouse, or complaining about the irritation he or she is in your life? What would your spouse say? Are you a champion or a critic?

One of the most important decisions you can make in your marriage is to see beyond yourself, your needs, and your feelings, and choose to be your partner's champion. Your husband or wife is a potential work of art. You participate with God and your spouse to create from the raw materials someone of enduring beauty. You do this through your attitudes, words, and actions.

"Instead of seeking new landscapes, develop new eyes."

Championing Through Attitudes

You can choose to notice your husband's strengths. You can choose to see your wife as God's gift to you. God has entrusted your spouse's heart to you. Does he or she feel your support? Know that you are on the same team? Goethe said, "Treat a man as he is, and he will remain as he is; treat a man as he can and should be, and he will become as he can and should be."

A friend of ours had a dream in which she saw her husband lying on an operating table in the hospital. She recognized the surgeon. He was none other than Jesus Christ.

Jesus turned and said to her, "You are with Me in this operating room. I am using you to bring healing into the life of your husband."

"Lord, what am I?" she asked. "Am I the scalpel? Are you using me to cut out my husband's malignancies?"

"No, that's not your use," Jesus replied. "Look again."

She scanned the operating theater. Could she be the heart machine, the operating table, the light? Each time she asked, the reply came back, "No, not that." Suddenly she saw something she hadn't seen before.

"Lord, am I the IV?"

"Yes, my child," He said. "I'm counting on you to keep the clear, life-building nourishment coming to this man you married."

With that our friend awakened. She was immediately aware that too many times she had seen it as her job to excise her husband's irritating habits and strange idiosyncrasies. Now the Lord was saying that she was supposed to provide emotional nourishment to her husband. How had she gotten into the habit of being the scalpel instead of the IV?

"It's time we used our head in order to save our heart."

Jesus brought the Gospel to us, the good news of unconditional love and acceptance. The Gospel took away condemnation, guilt, wrath, and supposedly, nagging. God, by accepting us, declares our value. He speaks His truth, but with an absence of condemnation and guilt. We need to champion our spouses the way He has championed us.

To share life with another person and to accept each other with ever-deepening understanding is the crowning glory of marriage. Championing sweeps away the distancing, destroying, degrading, and devaluing that is the result of our refusing to accept our marriage partners just the way they are.

The way you champion your mate, the way you respond to your mate, the way you free your mate, all these are ways you follow Jesus' example. Love always comes from a welcoming heart. It always has open arms. What is the ultimate symbol of open arms? It is Jesus Christ on the cross of Calvary. As His love connection to your world, and in particular to your spouse, can you refuse to open your arms, your thinking, and your loving?

Championing your spouse will cost you. If you are at home battling the kids, trying to get your own work done, facing a broken washing machine or a stalled car, it is rather easy to be upset that your wife is having such a good time in San Francisco. If she doesn't phone as much as you would like, you can label her a selfish ingrate. You can tell yourself that if she really loved you and was committed to the family, she'd hop on the next plane and come home. But if you are going to champion her, you will have to look at things differently and think differently.

Jesus champions us so we can champion others.

Here are some possible attitude adjustments that the husband described above could make:

I pride myself on freeing my wife to develop her talents in this way.

I get joy out of encouraging her growth.

I get tremendous fulfillment from making a contribution in my work. I'm sure she does too.

I am proud of her and what she is accomplishing.

If she doesn't call as much as I would like, I'll communicate that to her. I'll give her the benefit of the doubt. I'm sure she got caught up with work, colleagues, and friends.

I think we are both modeling healthy relationship to our children. There are times in every marriage when one person has to carry more of the load on the home front. I'm glad I can support her in this way. I'm glad there is room in our marriage for both of our interests and priorities.

When she comes back, after she gets rested, we'll have so much of interest to talk about and to share.

What a concept! Championing may require a real attitude adjustment on the part of both parties. One way to affect your own attitudinal change is to create a list of your spouse's gifts, talents, strengths, and the things you most appreciate. We have such a list that we keep in a private place. We attempt to add to it on a regular basis. When we have our individual quiet times, we pray through our lists, each of us thanking God for the high-quality person who has chosen to share this life with us.

You will be amazed at the difference this exercise of gratitude will make in your attitude, even on days when one of you is a little testy. There is another bonus, too! As we focus on what is good, our eyes are opened to see more.

In Ephesians 5 Paul tells the husband to love-treasure his wife and the wife to respect her husband—notice him, regard him, prefer him, and esteem him. Peter adds to this in his first letter (3:7), stating that each husband should live with his wife in a sensitive way—honoring her, serving her, and building her up. And more advice from Paul in Romans, "Love each other with genuine affection and take delight in honoring each other" (12:10, NLT), and in Philippians, "Fix your thoughts on what is true and good and right. Think about things that are pure and lovely, and dwell on the fine, good things in others. Think about all you can praise God for and be glad about" (4:8, TLB).

In South Africa, when they dig for diamonds, they move tons of earth to find a pebble not as large as a little fingernail. The miners are focused on the diamonds, not on the dirt. They have to move a lot of dirt to find one diamond.

In marriage, it is far too easy to shift our focus from the diamonds to the dirt. Yet Jesus always focused on the diamonds. He sees our intrinsic value and worth even when we're mucking around in the dirt. Can we do less if we are to be His love connection? Each of us needs to undergo a daily attitude check. We need to choose to see the unpolished diamonds and not to get distracted by the dirt.

One result of a regular attitude check will be self-restraint. There are times when the mature choice is to bite your tongue, rather than yelling biting words at your mate. You have a choice. Will you champion or crush your partner?

Championing Through Words

Does your spouse know that you are his or her number-one fan? It is not unusual for a couple to talk carelessly to and about each other. Sometimes we react destructively rather than speaking constructively.

As adults desiring to grow toward maturity, we choose to act rather than react. But acting is a conscious decision of the will. Choose words that are encouraging, loving, affirming, thoughtful, and considerate—whether you feel like it or not.

You can't do a lot about your spouse's behavior, but you can do a lot about your own. What happens in your home when one of you makes a mistake? Is the person encouraged or annihilated?

Speaking constructively, first of all, begins with noticing your spouse. How are you going to champion your husband if you haven't focused on him? Many of us haven't trained ourselves to be observant. Often we are preoccupied when we are with each other. No one wants to be invisible to the person he or she loves. The opposite of love is not hate; it is indifference. There is no rejection that hits us quite so deep as indifference from a spouse.

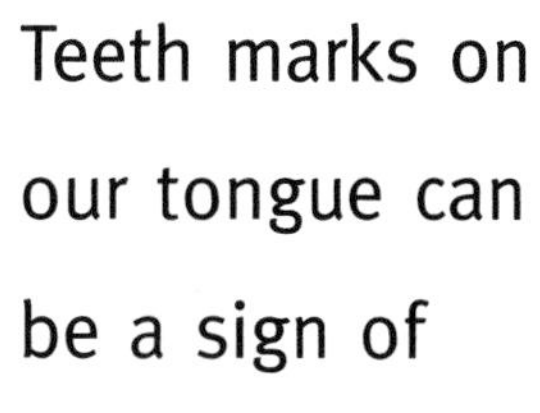

Teeth marks on our tongue can be a sign of maturity.

As God's love connection to our mates, we need to be constantly watching, listening, waiting, changing, adjusting, and readjusting. We are not today what we will be tomorrow. Each of us changes ever so subtly over the course of a day. If you fail to notice your spouse, you will surely miss the wonder of who he or she is becoming.

Jan: Some time ago Dave shaved off his mustache. It took me two days to notice. Following that embarrassing and comical moment, I made a covenant with the Lord to really notice Dave. Do you need to make such a pact?

It's not enough to just notice. We need to commit to taking the next step: choosing our words carefully.

Guys, keep the words coming:

"I love your body."

"I value your sensitivity."

"I love your smile."

"I'm proud of you."

We're not mind readers, but we can hear some of you now. You are probably thinking, I couldn't talk that way. I'm shy and I'd feel weird.

We are going to be bold and suggest that you change your attitude and vocabulary. You need to be willing to say, "I didn't use to talk this way, but now I do." Marriages don't just naturally grow; they naturally stagnate. Do you remember how much effort and thought you put into dating? Now that you're married, your "job" isn't over. You got the prize, now you have to be intentional about prizing the prize.

A very courageous husband gathered up all his bravado and approached his wife, "Honey," he asked her, "what's it like to live with me as your husband?"

His wife looked at him to see if he was serious. When she saw sincerity staring back at her, she said, "Well, you haven't said anything hurtful lately, but I can't remember the last time you said anything nice."

We interviewed a group of newlyweds to find out what their complaints were and were surprised by their responses. The major complaint was that their partners didn't give them enough verbal expression of affection. So later we did a little survey of our own. We asked some young men the words that would be music to their ears. They said:

"I'm proud of you."

"I love you."

"I want you now."

We have a feeling that there are many older men who long to hear the same words, and there is no doubt that a woman of any age longs to be championed in the same way.

When was the last time you championed your husband verbally? How long has it been since you told your wife how thrilled you are to be married to her? Do you elevate your husband when you talk to your family and friends? Do you refrain from saying unkind things to your wife when you are upset or tired? (Restraint is the utmost test of self-mastery.)

Bob Burg tells of an incident that left a huge impression on him. When he was twelve, carpet was being installed in their home. For lunch, his parents bought pizza for the crew. Dad went to talk with the boss, a stereotypical, beer-guzzling, hard-living guy, about the job. Bob was around the corner listening.

The boss said, "This is an expensive job. Women will really spend your money, won't they?"

"Well, I'll tell you," said Bob's dad, "when they were there with you before you had any money, it is a pleasure to do anything for them you possibly can."

This wasn't the answer the carpet installer expected to hear. "But don't women spend all they can?"

Bob's dad replied, "Hey, when they are the reason you are successful, you want them to do the things they enjoy. There is no greater pleasure." The crew boss tried one more time. "And they will take that as far as they can, huh?" His father responded, "She's the best thing that ever happened to me."

Finally the installer gave up and went back to work, probably shaking his head in bewilderment.

Bob said that witness-

notes

ing his dad in that moment taught him more about loving and respecting a wife than anything his father ever said directly about the subject.[1]

Words Spoken Ahead of Schedule

As amazing as it is, Jesus Christ, the Almighty God of the universe, champions each of us. We see this through the words He used in His first interaction with Simon Peter. When Jesus met Simon, He looked him straight in the eye and called him Peter. What is the difference, you ask? Simon means "reed," someone easily tossed to and fro. Peter means "rock," a symbol of stability.

Jesus did not withhold the name until Peter proved himself a man of stability. On the contrary, He spoke Peter's potential into being. Christ's words motivated Peter towards maturity. When we choose to champion our partners, we see them as they can become, not as they are at that moment. Words that champion motivate!

Don Quixote in *Man of La Mancha* slowly changes the self-concept of a prostitute by consistently and unconditionally speaking words of affirmation. He gives her a new name, Dulcinea, so that she will be reminded of her new identity. When she dares to believe his words, she acts differently. Words that champion impact our very identity!

Jesus Christ verbally champions each of us ahead of schedule. Instead of condemning us as sinners, He refers to us as saints and as children of God. That provides us with some growing space, doesn't it? It also serves as a warning. When we are upset and bring up each other's failures, each other's old identity, each other's faults, we are not championing each other. We are the voice of condemnation. We kill. We tear down. We destroy our mates' spirits.

The antidote for a poisoned spirit is to listen to honest words of affirmation from the person who committed to you for a lifetime. The person who loves you, believes in you, and champions you becomes an important source of your security. A true life mate is still with you even when you have given up on yourself.

Some of the greatest success stories have followed a word of encouragement or an act of confidence by a loved one. We have one of our own.

Jan: Dave was bogged down with the possibility of finishing his doctoral dissertation in time to graduate. He had spent almost five years pursuing this mutual goal of ours. I wasn't about to let him believe that he couldn't pull it off.

Together we discussed what would have to happen to make this dissertation a reality. Dave felt that he needed two weeks of uninterrupted study time away from school, home, and family. The arrangements were made, and a few moments before he was to leave, I went running up to him with a piece of paper in my hand. On it were printed these words:

You are invited to a
celebration dinner
honoring
Dr. David G. Congo
Saturday, May 28, 1983
Seven in the evening
at the home of
Janet and Dave Congo

After informing him that I had had twenty-five of these invitations printed up, I gave Dave a big hug and sent him off to finish his dissertation. Teasingly I told him that I knew he had a little Scottish blood in him and wouldn't want to waste the money!

Dave hugged me and thanked me for believing in him. And guess what? He finished. He graduated! During the next two weeks, my belief in him kept him going. "Your words kept me believing that I could do it, too," he says.

When we champion each other, we use words, powerful words, spoken ahead of schedule to encourage each other's spirit and to keep us believing in our dream. We bring out the best in each other.

Words Spoken Directly

One thing we learn from watching Christ's example is that words need to be spoken directly. Jesus didn't go to James and John to tell them about Peter's potential. He spoke directly to Peter.

Author John Powell was crying at his father's deathbed when a nurse tried to console him. He told the nurse that he was sad, but knew his father was prepared for death, due to his extended illness. "The reason I'm crying," said John Powell, "is that my father never told me he loved me."[2]

Have you told your partner recently that you love him or her? The best way to compliment one's spouse is frequently. We mustn't forget to champion our mates in public, but more importantly, we must believe in them and let them know in private as well. Speak words of love and affirmation directly to your husband or wife every chance you get.

Words Focused on Character

As we champion our spouses verbally, it becomes more powerful when we focus on how their actions reveal their character. Jesus, in His interaction with Simon Peter, could have focused just on Peter's actions or performance. He didn't. His words could have been, "You, Simon, will be an effective communicator, evangelist, or church planter." Instead, Jesus affirmed Peter's character and potential by saying, "You are a rock." This volatile fisherman was told that in his character he was stable. I wonder what Peter thought when he heard these words? Who me? No way. *I've sure got him fooled!* Or did he think, The me you see is the me I want to be.

We can both testify that when we are championed verbally, a transformation happens in us. It's as if we give each other not only acceptance but also confidence and strength. We end up saying, "My partner believes in me and what I can do. Maybe I can do it."

Each of us is significant and of great value in God's eyes because of what Jesus Christ accomplished on the cross. His love and affirmation are constant and unconditional. When a couple intentionally decides to champion one another, they unleash the power of love into their relationship. They become the channel of God's unconditional love and acceptance to each other.

Decision #5
"I Will Champion You"

For Reflection and Discussion

1. Do you need an attitude adjustment? Listed below are some championing attitudes. Put a check mark beside those attitudes that you are currently practicing in your marriage. Star those that you would like to adopt.

I will view you as a person, not a possession that I use in any way.

I will champion you as a person, even if I can't always champion your position.

I will believe in your potential. I will create a climate where growth is possible.

I will attempt to appreciate how our differences make us a better team.

I will choose to see the best in you.

I will be loyal to you at all times and especially when we are apart.

When I am tempted to belittle you in any way, I will stop myself.

I will encourage you by nurturing your leadership qualities.

In my heart, I will put you before my schedule, my work, my friends, my family, and even our children.

I will encourage you to develop your own interests.

I will be actively interested in what is important to you.

I will value it because you value it.

I will encourage you to develop relationships with friends who support our marriage.

I will be personally invested in your growth.

I will take more joy in giving to you than receiving from you.

I will be genuinely happy and supportive of your successes.

I will be genuinely empathetic when you fail.

I will make it safe for you to try something new.

I will be compassionate if you make a mistake.

I will listen to you with my heart and my eyes as well as my ears.

I will view problems as temporary. Our relationship and you will always be primary.

I will not give you a negative label. I will not stereotype, categorize, or prejudge you.

I will never give up on you.

I will thank God for you on a daily basis.

I will not ignore you as if you are invisible, a nonperson who doesn't exist.

2. Score yourself on the following scales:

I champion my spouse directly!

Rarely **Sometimes** **Never**

I champion my spouse ahead of schedule!

Rarely **Sometimes** **Never**

I champion my spouse by focusing on his or her character, not just performance!

Rarely **Sometimes** **Never**

3. Make a list of your spouse's strengths as described earlier in the chapter. Then make a list of what irritates you about your spouse. Now, we'd like to challenge you to run an experiment. Do not mention anything on your list of irritations to your husband or wife for an entire month. Instead, every day of the month, call attention to at least two items from your appreciation list. Let your mate discover that you are his or her number-one fan.

DECISION SIX

"I Will Nurture My Private Life"

Maurice and Sally have a recurring argument. Whenever Maurice wants time for himself or time with friends, Sally starts to pout. She views any separateness as a threat to their togetherness. Maurice frequently offers to give her some alone time and encourages her to go out with some girlfriends, but she never takes him up on his offer. She tries to make him feel guilty for wanting to do anything away from her and the family.

In contrast, the week prior to our wedding, our parents sat us down and talked to each of us about the importance of taking time for ourselves. To us this seemed like a contradiction; after all, we were focused on becoming one. We now see the wisdom of their advice.

Welcoming personal time into our marriage doesn't mean that we will end up as married singles unless we haven't settled the prior decision that our relationship will be a priority. Both men and women need time for themselves. We are not talking about the five minutes of peace and quiet you get in the bathroom (once a day if you are lucky). Separateness wisely used recharges our batteries.

Men may have more of a need for space and distance than women (although women need these also), but many don't know how to make their need known without hurting their wives. They may retreat into a noncommunicative shell, work late, or go out with the guys, leaving their wives feeling abandoned and alone.

Women, especially mothers, tell us that they find it nearly impossible to go from being a mother to being a lover if they haven't any time for just themselves. Self-time reduces stress, increases creativity, and seems to lessen their resentment about all the things they need to do.

When there is no separateness, both men and women are much more susceptible to the stinging effects of their day-to-day frustrations. Self-time is a buffering resource. Time alone brings a resiliency to their encounters with each other and with life.

Today, many couples are running themselves ragged. At the same time, they feel guilty that they aren't doing enough for their children. "Busy" has become a huge part of our identity. It's almost as if we need permission to take a break. We tremble to step off the treadmill for fear we'll lose our superhuman status.

Guilt and martyrdom keep us on the merry-go-round even when we're on vacation. *Fortune* magazine reported that eighty-two percent of American executives work while on their vacations.[1]

One of these executives, Greg Janoff, described his vacation routine with his family at a lakeside cottage. He would wake up early in the morning and go online at six-thirty to check his e-mail. Then he would check in with East Coast clients and customers. Next he would respond to the customers' requests. When that was done he would check his voicemail from the previous day and check his pager. Typically, in the middle of the day he'd check it all again. Then he'd go through the same routine right before the end of the day so he could stay on top of any requests coming from the West Coast. We're not sure his family was impressed with his dedication to his job.

When we nurture our private lives, our focus is more on being. Often, the resentment that partners feel over a lack of self-time makes its way into the bedroom and interferes with sexual desire. Husbands tell us that when their wives give them self-time, it is a gift. They come back refreshed, ready to give and more likely to extend more understanding toward their mates and their children. Since men generally need more space in a relationship than women do, encouraging one's husband to maintain a separate life is a very loving thing for a wife to do. Both husbands and wives are refreshed by their separateness.

> "No amount of human having or doing can make up for a deficit in human being."

The McCains' relationship is thriving. They met twenty-six years ago in high school. Their favorite date is still movies and a hamburger. It is the things they don't do together that are impacting their relationship.

After spending years at home raising their two daughters, Helen returned to school and now teaches English at a junior high. Brian is an administrator of a large clinic. One of his passions is car racing. He has some male buddies who share his passion. They plan three weekends away around major races. Helen's best friend is a sister who lives in another state. She and her sister schedule "girls' outings" on the same weekends. They love to explore new places together.

Once a year Brian and Helen spend a weekend with her sister and her husband in some new setting. Once a year Helen joins Brian at the races. Both partners are grateful that separateness is not a threat in their marriage. They feel energized by their weekends away, and the stories they share go on and on and on.

It is unhealthy to welcome your spouse's separate interests into your marriage while discouraging your own. Learning how to be

Respect . . . is appreciation of the seperateness of the other person, of the ways he or she is unique.

enriched by self-time is crucial. When separateness is fostered in your marriage, the more you have to bring to your relationship and the less tendency you will have to be needy. You won't demand things of your partner that he or she is incapable of or unwilling to give.

Warning: Choose to do nothing in your self-time that will threaten your relationship. The purpose of your self-time is to enrich your together time.

When we don't take time for personal renewal, fatigue leaves us feeling isolated and alienated. Laughter fades, as does creativity, and our tendency is towards self-absorption. Many people who get bored with their marriage are denying the sad reality that the emptiness is inside of them. People who haven't pursued self-understanding often blame their spouses and their marriage for their emptiness.

When we nurture our private selves, we are not expecting anyone or anything to fill our emptiness. We are accepting that we are responsible for that. In fact, this decision and taking responsibility for our own happiness are one and the same.

Choosing Your Attitude

Happiness is an inside job. No doubt almost all of us, at one point in time, thought it was our partners' job to make us happy. It usually doesn't take long to see that our mates have a tough time dealing with this attitude. It is a huge disappointment to accept the fact that no human being can bolster another's mood twenty-four hours a day. We can either take responsibility for our own state of being, or we can get furious and judge our mates for what we consider their inadequacy.

> Have you noticed yet that marriage doesn't make you happy? It makes you married. Happiness is up to you.

Many women report not being content. We imagine that men might receive a similar score. When we were children, our mothers were the secret to our state of mind. Very few mothers told us that personal happiness was our responsibility, so many of us fell into the habit of passively waiting . . . waiting for someone who would make us happy, someone who would bring life and excitement to our otherwise drab existence. Very subtly we started to believe that it was someone else's fault when we weren't happy. We pointed the finger at those who were letting us down, and we became victims. In addition to this, most women were raised to be caregivers, who believed they had the power to make someone happy, and most men were raised to be "care receivers," expecting someone to do that very thing. Is that a recipe for disaster or what!

It's fascinating that the "I'll-be-happy-when" philosophy eventually becomes an "I-was-happy-when." Many of us live the first half of our adult lives postponing satisfaction and the last half with regrets. But happiness is a personal journey, not a destination. We must choose to be happy. As the psalmist wrote, "This is the day the Lord has made; I will rejoice and be glad in it." There is an old Chinese proverb that says, "Happiness depends on something to work on, something to hope for, and someone to love."

Both partners are responsible to set the pace and tone of their home. Together they need to strive for a balance between their separateness and their togetherness. The decision to maintain a healthy life outside of marriage needs to be subordinate to the decision to make one's marriage relationship a priority.

Choosing Growth

When you are single, it is easy to accept that you are responsible for your own growth. That doesn't change just because you marry. We all operate best when we are well-rounded human beings. We are all responsible for taking care of our own physical, emotional, intellectual, and spiritual needs. The most loving thing you can do for your spouse is to take needed self-time to continue the process of growing into a whole person, the person God intended you to be.

It is necessary to ask yourself what you are doing on a regular basis to develop these four aspects of who you are. Is there more you would like to do? No spouse can make up for his or her mate's immaturity as a person. It's up to each of us to grow in maturity. Then we bring that maturity to our marriage.

We need to learn:
To be vulnerable and share our own feelings
To be assertive
To value the feelings, thoughts, and attitudes of the other
To have a life apart from the person we love
To allow our partners to be different
To say no
To hear no and respect it
To be real
To accept imperfections in our spouses and ourselves
To think for ourselves and express our own opinions
To take risks
To be responsible and follow through
To face our own selfishness
To have an intellectual life
To develop a sense of morality
To be spiritual
To be sexual
To discover and use our talents
To have a minimal amount of organization
To grieve

If you've ever felt that your marriage is benefiting your spouse far more than you, it's possible that you have been living for your partner at the expense of developing yourself. Marriage is about self-sacrifice, but not about other-absorption. You don't want to be like the chameleon that climbed onto a plaid jacket and suffered an enormous identity crisis! If you have abandoned self-development and live only for your mate, you are left miserable, fearful, and confused.

We visited a dear young couple just starting out. As we were enjoying their company, the husband said, "You know, there is only going to be one star in this family." We were shocked. He was just beginning a pastoral ministry, and his philosophy was that his wife was there to make him the star. He expected her to set aside her dreams and development to help him make a name for himself.

> "Marriage is about self-sacrifice, but not about other-absorption."

Unfortunately, or maybe fortunately for them, he made his pronouncement to the wrong couple. We suggested that Jesus needed to be the "star" in their marriage, and they needed to be totally dedicated to championing each other's growth and development.

The fantasy some bring into marriage is that their spouses will care for them so they don't have to care for themselves. That is a formula for disaster. No other human being can think for you, feel for you, or give your life meaning.

On our wedding day none of us has a corner on the maturity market. Instead we are in the process of growing toward maturity. The truth is we have TMMs—Temporary Moments of Maturity. One of Groucho Marx's friends gave him this advice prior to his engagement. "She is a lovely woman. She deserves a good husband. Marry her before she finds one." Seriously, it takes two mature adults to create a marriage.

Sometimes the most wonderful thing you can do for your relationship is to take some time off to renew yourself, as long as you have made the commitment that nothing you do in your separateness will in any way threaten or destroy your togetherness. Your individual growth needs to happen because of the relationship, not at the expense of the relationship. The continued development of your uniqueness is important to your marriage.

Quality of life comes from the inside out. That is God's way of growing us. Each of us needs to take time to nurture our soul. This is not your spouse's job or responsibility. You need time to have authentic connection with God, your friends, and with yourself.

Choosing to Quest after God

Regardless of what all the love songs say, it's not love or even marriage that gives us a purpose for living—our faith does. In the Gospel of Mark we read what Jesus calls the highest quest: "Love the Lord your God with all your heart and with all your soul and with all your mind and with all your strength" (12:30). Your marriage must take second place to your pursuit of God. And your quest for God is not your spouse's responsibility, but your own.

Over the years, though, we have come to see that we cannot say that we are pursuing God with our whole heart and at the same time be half-hearted in our commitment to each other. Marriage is the primary context that God uses to teach us about ourselves, and also about love, forgiveness, joy, hope, and suffering. He wants to be invited daily into every aspect of our lives and hearts.

In many ways, our marriage is a byproduct of our quest to know God. Perhaps when we are really upset with our mates, we don't want to face our need for change, but reading the Scripture can change our perspective if we are open to God's direction. One husband told God that he would treat his wife with the kindness of Christ—not because she deserved it, but because Christ deserved it. In the process, he was transformed, and his wife blossomed.

The Christian walk is not about imitation but habitation. We need time alone with Jesus on a daily basis if we are committed to a spiritual quest. We must be God-centered. Pant after God's own heart, and let Him find you.

Christ pulled away from the crowds in order to quest after God. Below are some verses that encourage us to do the same.

"Very early in the morning, while it was still dark, Jesus got up, left the house and went off to a solitary place, where he prayed" (Mark 1:35).

"But Jesus often withdrew to lonely places and prayed" (Luke 5:16).

Even though Jesus "lived and moved and had his being in God," He still shut the world out for large chunks of time in order to have uninterrupted time of communication with His Father.

"And without faith it is impossible to please God, because anyone who comes to him must believe that he exists and that he rewards those who earnestly seek him" (Hebrews 11:6).

"You will keep in perfect peace him whose mind is steadfast, because he trusts in you" (Isaiah 26:3).

"You have made known to me the path of life; you will fill me with joy in your presence, with eternal pleasures at your right hand" (Psalm 16:11).

With Augustine we can affirm that "our hearts are restless, O God, until they rest in Thee." Learning to live life from the inside out is possible only when we pause regularly to nurture a deep inner life and to allow our quiet times to transform us.

Will we allow God to use our marriages to change us? Are we willing to adjust to what God requires of us? Love challenges us to break our fixation with ourselves. In order to bring another into our life in love, we must be willing to give up certain destructive characteristics.

The need to be always right.
The need to be first in everything.
The need to be constantly in control.
The need to be perfect.
The need for them to be perfect.
The need to be loved by everyone.
The need to possess.

The need to be free of conflict and frustration.
The need to change others for our needs.
The need to manipulate.
The need to blame.
The need to dominate.[2]

It's easy to deceive yourself about how your behavior affects your spouse. It's easy to deceive yourself about your own fears. It's easy to push, prod, argue, justify, defend, withdraw, and blow up so that your will will be done. It's easy to let your limitations become the limitations of the marriage. It's easy to let your self-centeredness permeate your marriage. It's easy unless you step back and surrender your will to His will on a regular basis. It's easy unless you study His heart and grieve that yours is so cold. It's easy unless you "guard your heart, for it is the wellspring of life" (Proverbs 4:23).

When you intentionally nurture the spiritual dimension of your private life, it gives you a sense of meaning and purpose that powerfully impacts your daily decisions. You live with the big picture in mind—from the perspective of eternity. It becomes the source of your passion for living and for loving.

Gordon Dahl writes, "When we fail to nurture our spiritual self and to cultivate a rich inner life, there are dues to pay relationally. Most middle-class Americans tend to worship their work, to work at their play, and to play at their worship. As a result, their meanings and values are distorted. Their relationships disintegrate faster than they can keep them in repair, and their lifestyles resemble a cast of characters in search of a plot."[3]

Choosing to Connect with Friends

It puts too much pressure on a husband when a wife expects him to meet all of her emotional needs. Women need other women to discover the essence of their true femininity. Likewise men need other men to discover the essence of their true masculinity. Same-sex friendships bring great joy and solace to our private lives.

Dick and Roy had shared a friendship for over thirty years. Their conversations centered on work and sports. But they never talked about feelings, hopes, or dreams. About a year ago, Roy had to have back surgery. He was anxious and intimidated by the experience ahead of him. Roy's wife, Sue, sensed that he needed his old friend. She called Dick to let him know how frightened and alone Roy was feeling on the eve of his operation.

Dick left for the hospital as soon as he could. On the way he bought fifty dollars' worth of Italian food. He had a Merry Christmas paper tablecloth and napkins with him. It wasn't Christmas, but that happened to be all he could find at home.

You can imagine Roy's delight when his buddy entered his room. The aromas were intoxicating. Soon Dick had turned Roy's bed into an Italian feast. They laughed, talked, and prayed until the wee hours of the morning, even though Dick had to fly to Denver on a business trip in just a few hours. When Roy suggested that Dick leave early, his reply was that sleep was overrated.

Roy had his surgery, and everything went fine. A few weeks later Dick received a card. It said:

Dear Dick,
I know we have been friends for a long time. I've always wanted to tell you something, but I guess I always held myself back. I love you, bud. Thanks for everything you've done for me.
Roy

Dick still chokes up when he thinks about that card. He says he'll save it until they bury him.

Isolation from friends can cause you to be too emotionally dependent on your spouse and make you overly sensitive to any perceived abandonment or rejection on his or her part. It's as if your partner is the only pillar around which your self-esteem is built. Isolation also leads to a marriage in which one or both expect far too much from the other. But your spouse is not God. One person can never be all you need in life.

Some couples can't seem to have a conversation without one of them bringing up some unmet need. In fact, they seem to have a competition over who has the most. Eventually each believes that the other is a tremendously heavy burden. Why? Because neither is taking any responsibility for getting his or her own needs met.

A circle of friends can round out your life. They provide an emotional outlet. Your shared history is a treasured part of who you are. Your friends know your strengths and your weaknesses and yet they accept you.

All of us need deep, sustaining, healing, and supportive emotional relationships. We need friends who are committed to holding us accountable to grow. Sometimes we need friends who help us become whole enough to be able to get closer to our spouses. These kinds of friends don't threaten our commitment to our marriage, instead they enrich our lives and our marriages.

When you are connected to friends who are committed to your marriage's survival, they help you face your part in any problem (instead of just agreeing with you that truly your mate must be from a different planet). They encourage you to deal with the problem. As you learn to accept and trust your friends, your support group, or your counselor/mentor, this carries over into your marriage. It's been said that "a friend is a gift you give yourself." That is so true. A friend is also a gift you give your marriage.

Choosing a Quality of Life

Quality of life is an inside-out phenomenon. We all benefit when we take time to nurture our inner lives. Once again we want to stress that this is not your partner's responsibility. Each of us needs to take the time to have an authentic connection with ourselves.

Who are you, apart from your role as husband or wife? What are your values? What are you feeling? What is important to you? What do you want? What do you need?

If you can't answer these questions, you have slipped into being an invisible nonperson. A prerequisite to marital intimacy is that both partners know themselves. Often when we make the commitment of marriage, we fear that our individual dreams, our tastes, our separateness, will die. That does not need to be our fear, because it takes two separate individuals to create a relationship of love.

Choosing to Pursue Our Dreams

Many of us had personal dreams we shelved when we met, fell in love, got married, and began to have children. Some of you can barely remember what they were. Perhaps it's time for you to dust those off again and try them on for size. Please don't hold back for fear of being ridiculed, misunderstood, or ignored. Sometimes dreams come true, sometimes they don't. Regardless, pursuing your dream will give meaning and purpose to your life.

God abhors sameness. Every flower in the field is unique, as is every snowflake. No two roses are identical, even if among the same variety. Our fingerprints and our DNA are unique to the degree that others can identify us by them. Yet often we are threatened by diversity. Either we distance from it or we try to force uniqueness into sameness. Only then do we feel secure.

We suggest that instead you welcome and celebrate the diversity in your marriage. Oh, there will be times when you are irritated by it, but most of the time your marriage will be enriched by it. Each of us needs to discover the many possibilities that lie dormant within us. If we stop fighting it, our separateness and our uniqueness will add depth and breadth to our marriage.

What gives you pleasure? What gives you a sense of fulfillment? If you have abandoned these things because you are married, you have fundamentally abandoned yourself.

Choosing a Plan

Do you honor the commitments you make to others, but ignore the ones you make to yourself? If so, consider an attitude adjustment. At first you may find yourself uncomfortable or feeling guilty about allowing yourself personal time. Don't be hard on yourself. Allow yourself to feel uncomfortable. We promise you that eventually your anxious feelings will be replaced by feelings of anticipation. Whatever you do, don't start in on unfinished chores when you finally get some time for yourself.

If you have young children and rarely find yourself with the luxury of an empty house or free time, trade baby-sitting with a friend so you both can enjoy some time for yourselves. Some couples arrange to have a sitter come in on Saturday morning so they both can go separate ways and have time alone.

As we have mentioned, we sit down with our calendar once a week. In addition to scheduling date times and physical intimacy times, we schedule our separateness. Other couples we have interviewed take turns facilitating the other's self-time. Obviously equal amounts may not always be possible. Some weeks you may get more, some less. Make it a priority to see that you are both enjoying separate time.

Jan says: One Christmas years ago, when we had two precious babies and were short of cash, Dave gave me the most incredible gift. He gave me the gift of one hour a day in which I could have self-time. Talk about the gift that keeps on giving. I can give testimony to the fact that separateness, wisely used, recharges our love batteries.

Frank and Diane have taken their appreciation of each other's need for separateness to a new level. They each have one room in their home that is their sanctuary. They have decorated this space with things that are precious to them: photographs of people who have influenced them, books they are enriched by, hobbies they enjoy, colors they delight in, and music they love. They were both active in helping each other create their space. In the process, they report, they learned so much about each other.

Perhaps you don't have two entire rooms available for you to celebrate your uniqueness in, but what about two corners?

Every developmental change in a couple's life may require a new approach to the balance between separateness and togetherness. Newlyweds need a great deal of shared time to consolidate their marriage relationship. Older married couples, while making their relationship a priority, may prefer to use more of their leisure time in independent activities.

Taking responsibility to nurture your private life so that you are feeling gratitude for a life full of meaning and purpose translates into bringing a fulfilled self to the marriage relationship. We can't think of a nicer gift to give your partner.

But let there be spaces in your togetherness,
And let the winds of heaven dance between you. . . .
Fill each other's cup but drink not from one cup.
Sing and dance together and be joyous, but let each
one of you be alone . . .

- *Kahlil Gibran*[4]

If you don't work at becoming two, it will be impossible for you to become one as God intended.

Decision #6
"I Will Nurture My Private Life"

For Reflection and Discussion

1. What fills you up? What brings you joy?
   What refuels you?
2. What is in your separate circle that nurtures you and benefits your marriage?

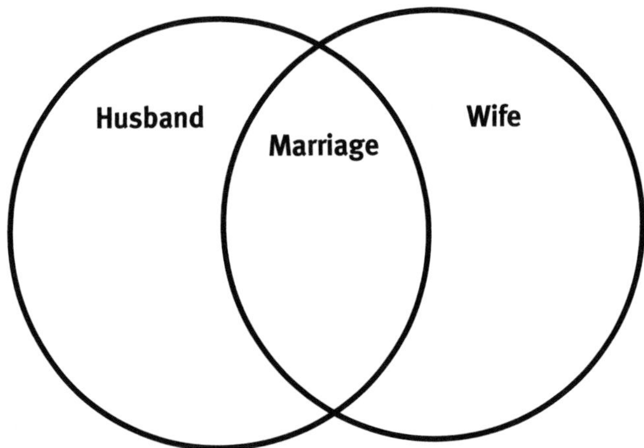

3. Complete these sentences.
   As a child, I believed that taking time for myself was . . .
   My mother believed self-time was . . .
   My father believed it was . . .
   I think my LifeMate believes it is . . .
   Today, if I ever take time for myself I feel . . .
   The last thing I did for myself was . . .
4. Have you stopped valuing who God made you to be? When was the last time you took any time to develop yourself?
5. List here some possible options for self-time:

DECISION SEVEN

"I Will Be Responsible and Reliable"

Once at a Family Life Conference that we were leading, we had an encounter with an amazing couple, Pastor Keith and Mary Korstjens. It was impossible not to be affected by this couple's love for each other.

Over the weekend they shared their story with us. One Saturday in October 1955, Keith, a new husband of three years, watched in disbelief as Mary's attempts to raise herself up on her elbow completely failed. Helplessly she crumpled onto their mattress.

Keith, heart pounding, rushed this beautiful, twenty-four-year-old love of his life to the hospital. He spent six agonizing hours waiting in the emergency room only to be told that she had polio. Mary would be a quadriplegic for the remainder of her life.

What in the world did we, as a young couple, have to teach this couple? Absolutely nothing! They were gracious enough not to tell us that. When we weren't presenting, we were sitting at Keith and Mary's feet trying to learn from them.

Twenty-six years after that Saturday morning that forever changed their lives, Keith and Mary told their story in a book called *Not a Sometimes Love*. Keith and Mary are honest about how radically this diagnosis changed their lives. They both can laugh at some of their experiences, but they also share the depth of their despair.

When Keith was told that he could bring Mary home for her first visit from the hospital, he prepared for days. He had a friend act as a chauffeur because his friend's car was easier to get into. He had forgotten one item, however—a bedpan. When Mary realized that she might not have what she needed if she dared go home, she couldn't win her battle over fear and panic. Keith had to take her back to the hospital. Can you imagine how terrifying that experience must have been for both of them? It was only later that he learned that Saturday was the first time Mary had even been on a portable respirator. She wasn't sure that she could trust that battery-operated machine or her young husband.

The next Saturday he tried again. He parked the car in the same place at the hospital. Mary was wheeled down to the waiting car. Then came the moment of truth, when Keith had to lift her from the wheelchair to the car. While in the wheelchair, Mary was attached to the battery-powered, portable respirator by a long vacuum-cleaner-type hose. The hose had to be disconnected while the machine was placed inside the car. In his mind, Keith had practiced this procedure thousands of times, but could he do it now? He had to disengage the hose, move the heavy respirator and battery pack into the back of their car, and reattach the hose to his wife's body unit all in time. Fighting panic, he prayed for steadiness. Mary let out a heartrending little cry, "Oh, honey, hurry!" He couldn't make a mistake. The hose was connected, and Mary was breathing in rhythm with the machine again. As Keith closed the car door on Mary's side and walked to the driver's side, his knees were trembling uncontrollably. Could he do this?

Day after day, night after night, they've done it. There have been questions and moments of heart-wrenching frustration. There have been times when the million small indignities and inconveniences felt too heavy to bear.

Mary required total personal care. Frequently Keith was the only one available to care for her toileting needs. He was the one who had to get up multiple times each night to check the pressure on the respirator, to get the bedpan, to tend to the children. His work as a pastor took him out of their home several evenings a week. Mary was totally dependent upon someone's assistance twenty-four hours a day. One can only imagine how difficult it would be to find competent help.

Keith says that the greatest unanswered prayer in their lives has been the prayer for adequate help. He writes:

> So I have this little plan. I struggle out of bed about thirty minutes before I intend to help Mary up. I grope my way into the bathroom to shower and shave. This helps me achieve some degree of humanness again, and then I go to the kitchento fix our breakfast. While the coffee is perking, I go back up to help Mary from our bed into the bathroom. While she's there I go back into the bedroom, make the beds, and put away the respirator and shell. Next, out to the kitchen we go for breakfast. Afterwards, the dishes get rinsed and stacked in the dishwasher. Finally, I'm ready to take Mary back into the bathroom to bathe and dress her. Then I put on my tie and coat and we're off to take her to someone's home for the day. It's a great schedule. If I keep on it, we can do beautifully.
>
> But do you know what? Sometimes I hate that schedule!Sometimes I get fed up with the routine. But something happens somewhere in the middle of my whispered conversation with God while I'm straightening the bedspread. I'm muttering to Him about how grim this all is—and how unfair I think it is that we don't have a housekeeper—and He alwayslets me know He still accepts me, even with my complaining. He sort of smiles and says, "Sure, I know, you're a little bent out of shape this morning, and you want to feel

crummy for awhile. That's okay. I can handle that all right. Go ahead and get it outof your system and then let's get on with the day."[1]

Can any of us comprehend for even one moment how difficult and challenging life would be in a relationship that required such great one-sided sacrifice? Our lives, as we know it, would be forever changed. Only a few couples have to face the kind of stark reality that Mary and Keith had to face so early in their marriage journey. So how does commitment in everyday life play itself out on the small screen?

Even in "ordinary" circumstances, marriage requires more of us than we are often comfortable giving. All of us at times are torn between our dream of a deeply gratifying marriage and the reality of what that relationship requires. Marriage requires sacrifice of all of us. The skills of total self-reliance and independence are skills that help us to divorce, not marry. Some of our individual preferences and rights need to be sacrificed.

Commitment for Jesus began when He surrendered His personal rights. He left the wonder of heaven. He left His position at the right hand of the Father to come to earth to become a man. Someone has penned these words about our amazing Savior:

> Because we children of Adam wanted to become great,
> He became small.
> Because we would not stoop, He humbled himself.
> Because we wanted to rule, He came to serve.

How does this commitment work in the day-to-day life of a married couple?

Start Being an Adult

Ralph has anticipated marriage since he was in his late teens. His parents had enjoyed their own relationship, and that had inspired their only son. His mother had been the ultimate stay-at-home mom. She was a fantastic cook, a creative homemaker. Nothing had been expected on the home front of either Ralph or his father. As a result, Ralph's fantasy of a wife is of an idealized mother who lives to give him constant validation and affirmation while at the same time picking up after him. He dreams of a beautiful woman who will meet his every need.

Ralph isn't alone. How many young women enter marriage expecting their husbands to be idealized father figures who dote on their little princesses and provide unlimited cash for every whim? Many women were raised to be a beautiful centerpiece of whom nothing but beauty and charm were expected.

If as an adolescent you were raised by a mom or dad who acted as your human safety net, choosing to be an adult is going to be extremely challenging. What adulthood requires of you will seem unfair. After all, growing up you rarely, if ever, felt anxiety about anything. You didn't have to, because your parents got in the way of any logical consequences and rarely enforced any rules. Nothing was expected of you.

notes

They'd be at the computer typing your papers all night before they were due because you needed your sleep. If you ran out of cash because you had made an impulsive decision, they would open their wallets. Mom or Dad might ask for your help with some chores, but if you complained enough, they'd back right off because they wanted you to be happy. Your assumption is that love and rescuing are synonymous. Someone has always been there to pick up the pieces and clean up the messes. You expect your spouse to continue this pattern and keep your life anxiety free.

Parents who do not encourage their children's reliable and responsible behavior do a terrible disservice both to the children and to their future mates.

Ideally marriage yokes us together in an adult relationship so that we can work together to create a life for ourselves and for our precious children that honors and glorifies the God we serve. Adults anticipate being yoked with other adults who bring home a paycheck, file their income taxes on time, stick to a budget, and who help with chores. If one person in the marriage does not accept the responsibilities of being an adult, the relationship starts to decay.

It was a second marriage for Jake and Elaine. Both had children from previous relationships. Jake only got to see his son every other weekend, while Elaine's daughter lived with them. On weekends when Jake's son was due to visit, neither Jake nor his ex-wife was willing to go out of the way to get him to his dad's home. In fact, it was not unusual for Jake to play golf all day and expect Elaine to go two hours out of her way to pick up his son. When Elaine raised this as an issue, Jake called her selfish and did his best to make her feel guilty for not caring for his son as she did for her daughter. In addition, he talked to his mother and father about how inconsiderate his new wife was. Instead of confronting their son's irresponsibility, they teamed up with him against Elaine.

If, like Jake, one mate is not an adult in the marriage, he or she may experience the spouse as a disapproving parent. The Apostle Paul used these words to challenge the Corinthian believers to grow up (it's fascinating that they are found in the middle of his admonition to love with a mature love): "When I was a child, I talked like a child, I thought like a child, I reasoned like a child. When I became a man, I put childish ways behind me" (1 Corinthians 13:11).

Adults rely on each other. We team together to get the tasks of married life done. Marriage requires two adults who each stroke the oars so that their boat doesn't go around in circles. However some husbands and wives aren't even good roommates, let alone life mates.

Stop Being a Victim

Since Adam and Eve, we as humans have fantasized about someone taking responsibility for us. We dream about a life without consequences. It just doesn't seem fair that we have to be personally responsible.

Sean would get together to play basketball with his buddies every Saturday morning. He loved this time. In fact, some weeks the thought of that game pulled him through his workweek. His wife, Janine, understood his need to be with his basketball friends, and she supported his recreation. Eventually, though, her frustration began mounting. Sean would promise her that he would be available to his young family at 11:30 on Saturday morning, then he wouldn't show up until 2 or 3 p.m. His excuse was always the same: "The time just got away from me."

Janine loved Sean, but she hated broken promises. She hated organizing her day around a promise, only to see their plans collapse time and again. She waited and carefully chose the time when she would raise the issue with Sean. She expressed her frustration with the predicament his broken promises created. She set a boundary. She told him that she and the children would anticipate his return at 11:30 on Saturday. If he chose not to be there when he promised, they would go on with the planned activities of the day without him.

Sean raged at her for her selfishness. He accused her of trying to put a wedge between him and the children. He felt perfectly justified. After all, she knew how hard he worked to support the family during the week. In his anger, he neglected to admit that she also worked to help support their family. Janine very wisely didn't get sidetracked on that point. Instead she expressed her love for him, affirmed his hard work for the family, and restated her position. If he couldn't keep his promise, she and the children would continue the day as planned.

Sean stormed out and went right over to his basketball buddy's house. He proceeded to let his friend know what a nag Janine was, how unreasonable she was being, and how unfair her policy was. He felt like a victim. He'd married a witch!

Sean found it easy to be a martyr because his expectation was that Janine would adopt the stance his mother had taken over the years. His mother had just sighed and put up with his father. She saw herself as a constant victim. She got sympathy in that role. Sean's father believed promises were made to be broken. The only problem Sean had was that Janine was not as enamored as Sean was by his family's way of doing things.

The victim role is a dangerous position to take because in order to adopt it, you have to totally disregard your part in the equation. You have to focus on the speck in your partner's eye rather than admitting that there is a log in your own.

If it is obvious to others that your spouse is irresponsible and unreliable, it is far too easy to get sympathy. But sympathy doesn't do you a lot of good. It helps you to feel resentful and superior. Instead, like Janine, you need to speak your truth in love, set your limits, and establish consequences.

Start with the Little Things

The actor Sylvester Stallone was being interviewed on television one evening. The host very straightforwardly expressed his awareness that Stallone no longer commanded the superstar status that he had earlier in his career and during his first marriage. Sylvester agreed with the host's perception and then went on to say, "I was getting big strokes for my ego back then, but now my priorities have changed. I'm in a wonderful relationship, and I have wonderful children. I've come to realize it's the little strokes every day that create a masterpiece, not the big ones."

Little things mean a lot. Little things create the masterpiece we call our life. Irresponsibility and unreliability destroy that masterpiece. Little things mean . . .

. . . I Can Trust You

Researchers have identified trust as a much greater predictor of positive marital outcome than love.[2] Tasks in marriage provide the stage on which trust and a sense of reliability are built. How spouses fulfill their obligations to each other demonstrates how much they trust each other.

When you feel as if you are carrying the major load in your marriage, you feel disappointed and cheated. Anxiety sets in. You start to believe that your life partner is not committed to meeting your needs and is taking advantage of you. At that point, if you don't address the problem and set boundaries, the temptation is to give less and less and to try to force the other to do his or her part, using whatever tactics are necessary. In contrast, when you know that you are not doing your part, you have to fight off feelings of guilt. You know you are unreliable. Your sense of self is diminished.

When the loving sacrifice in a marriage is mutual, trust grows. If trust is high, then you freely give to the relationship out of love, not duty, knowing that your partner will reciprocate in a responsible way. In a marriage of high trust, it is obvious to both partners that their needs will be met by the relationship. Both are considered valid and important. As a result they can relax. Their sense of justice is satisfied. They trust one another and feel safe in their marriage.

. . . I Respect You

When a couple's "us" comes up with a plan for money management, chores, or parenting, and then one partner doesn't follow through, the other feels betrayed, invisible, disappointed, disrespected . . . diminished. Without mutuality of sacrifice it's not really a marriage, it's more of a master-slave relationship. This kind of a relationship has all the disadvantages of marriage but none of the advantages. Once again, it breeds distrust.

One woman expressed her frustration over the inequity in her relationship. "My husband and I have a huge inequality when it comes to our leisure time. He works full time away from home; I work part-time and in addition handle virtually all the housework and child care except for car maintenance and outdoor Saturday chores. I have to get up earlier to get him and the kids ready for the day. He has time to play with our kids. In the evenings when he's settled down to watch TV, I'm still paying the bills or folding laundry. He takes his leisure when he wants or needs it, but I don't have that luxury. Is this pattern a wife's role, and should I just stop complaining about it? It's hard not to be resentful."[3]

. . . We're a Team

Men and women need to step up to the plate. If any of us had coworkers who expected us to do all of their work as well as our own, we would be upset. Yet that is the attitude many have when it comes to marriage.

One research study reported that women in two-income families spend an extra four months on household work than men do in any given year.[4] In addition to helping produce income for the family's survival, these women do most of the household tasks and carry the majority of the child-care responsibilities. Their husbands prefer to do home repair, car maintenance, and lawn care. Rarely do they do household chores. If they do, they refer to their contribution as "helping" their wives with their responsibilities. No wonder working wives and mothers are more likely than any other group to experience anxiety, chronic exhaustion, depression, low sex drive, and feelings of apprehension.[5]

The major contribution of some husbands is to create more work for their wives. We hope that is not true of you.

> The American male's lifestyle resembles something out of zoology—a juvenile phase during which we are cared for our mothers; a short free-swimming interlude where we semi-care for ourselves, and a mature phase where we once again resume our place being cared for by females we love.
> —James Thornton

As one man said, "There isn't man's work or woman's work. There is just work and too much of it." Terry Hargrave, a researcher and author, suggests that there are two kinds of work that are necessary for the smooth functioning of a marriage. There is the work that provides the necessary income for the marriage, and the work that accomplishes the everyday functional and emotional tasks that allow the "us" to thrive.[6]

If your expectation is that your spouse should do more or less because that's what happened in your family of origin, maybe it is time for you to return to the drawing board. You need to create an "us" that is different from your parents', your pastor's, or your neighbor's. Don't let someone else determine the rules and the roles for your marriage; instead, make choices. The question you must ask as a couple is, "How will this work best for the two of us?"

Hargrave goes on to suggest that the work of marriage needs to be decided through negotiation and choice. We believe that household tasks need to be divided around skills and deficits rather than gender.

Men are a tremendous resource to the family. Research has validated that men who do housework are healthier psychologically and are better able to deal with conflict and emotional intimacy with their wives.[7]

Women are a tremendous resource to the family. Women need to learn to let go of some of the tasks that they have been shouldering and open themselves up to another way of doing these tasks—their husbands' way.

Love manifests itself through action. Indeed, love is an action, and not a feeling. Jesus commanded us to love our enemies. Emotions can't be commanded. If Christ is Lord, He can command my will, my decision process, and my actions. Love involves self-denial. There are times when we must push our feelings into the background in order to live up to our commitments.

"We need to remind ourselves that no loving action ever contradicts any of God's commandments."

. . . I Can Depend on You

Broken promises do more damage than no promise at all. What security and safety comes to your spirit when you can depend upon your partner to do what he or she has promised, when your partner's word is as good as gold.

Perfection isn't necessary, but consistent reliability is. A couple can relax when both know that to the best of their ability, their partners will stay within their agreed-upon budget, will come home when they say they will or they will call, will stay sexually faithful, and will complete all chores as promised. When both partners keep the commitments they make, both are set free to pursue their dreams, confident in each other's love and dependability.

. . . A Daily Choice

Don't shower me with love and kisses. Just whisper softly, "I'll do the dishes."

This is where the rubber hits the road in a marriage. When couples accomplish the tasks of life together, they free up time to pursue personal and marital goals. This enriches their enjoyment of their relationship and each other.

Athletes have to practice their fundamentals, whether they have an audience or not and whether they feel like it or not. They do the mundane things when no one is looking. They have to fight through all the times when it's just plain work. What athlete wouldn't like to take a break from those fundamentals? Yet they become tremendously important in the fourth quarter of a football game.

If we are investing in making our lifetime relationship mutually beneficial, the little things, the fundamentals, the draining things, have to be accepted every day. Paul challenges each of us to offer our bodies "as living sacrifices, holy and pleasing to God" (Romans 12:1). In the same passage he writes, "Do not think of yourself more highly than you ought, but rather think of yourself with sober judgment" (v. 3).

James made a good living for his little family of three. Together he and his young wife, Lisa, had decided that when they started a family Lisa would be a stay-at-home mom. She left her career to raise their children two months before their first child was born. Over the past couple of years, however, Lisa has felt increasingly devalued by her husband. It appears to her that he thinks she plays all day. It is true that she has more choice schedule-wise than James does. She can work a women's Bible study and a weekly tennis game in among the cleaning, cooking, chauffeuring, and grocery shopping, while his work setting doesn't afford him that freedom.

If Lisa asks him to assist her with any tasks, James' response is increasingly sarcastic. He seems to insinuate that she is inept because she hasn't accomplished everything on her list. When he does help, he grumbles and complains all the way through the task. Lisa finds his attitude torturous to endure. The final straw happened at a Christmas party at James' place of employment, when he cracked a joke in front of Lisa and an attractive female coworker that demeaned homemakers.

Lisa was hurt and angry. As they were driving home, she told James that she was too upset to discuss the incident at that time. She asked him to set an appointment for the next day when they could talk about his comment. She asked him to be prepared to finish this sentence for her at that time. The sentence was, "If I were to admit that what you do is work, I . . ."

When they sat down the next day, James had both a different attitude and an entirely different perspective. He had taken his wife's assignment seriously. The first thing he did was to apologize to Lisa for the putdown he had slammed at her the night before. Then he said, "I resented the sentence completion assignment, but it also haunted me. I woke up early this morning with it on my mind, and I think I've clarified a few issues in my thinking." With that he handed her a paper on which he'd written the following:

> If I were to admit that what you do is work . . .
> . . . I'd be more willing to help you.
> . . . I'd express my gratitude regularly.
> . . . I'd acknowledge that you make my life easier.
> . . . I'd be amazed at your stamina.
> . . . I'd understand your exhaustion.
> . . . I'd see how mundane many of the tasks you have to complete are.
> . . . I'd understand some of your frustration.
> . . . I'd see your need for a creative outlet.
> . . . I'd change my attitude that I'm the only one doing anything valuable because my work has a paycheck attached to it.

. . . I'd ask God to forgive my arrogance.

James and Lisa reached for each other. Lisa thanked him for taking her request seriously. Lisa acknowledged the load James carried at work. She expressed gratitude for his faithfulness to the family financially. She expected to do more of the chores, at this life stage, because she was at home with the children. Together they decided to make a "Chores Are a Bore" chart. What chores would James willingly take on as his responsibility? Together they decided to try their plan for one month and then review it.

James also had a request. He asked Lisa not to comment on his cleaning style unless he asked her for advice. He said, "I hate getting busted for not doing it your way. It brings up feelings I had as a little boy when my mother got upset at the state of my room." Lisa agreed to set him free to do it his way. Then she asked, "What do we do if we forget to do what we promised?"

After a few moments, James came up with a plan. "I think the person needs to apologize because they've let the team down. Then I think he or she needs to do one chore on his or her partner's list." They shook on that agreement.

This conversation was a turning point in their relationship. Once a month they reevaluate if their plan is still working for them. With each stage of life and as more children have entered the family, the "Chores Are a Bore" list has been revamped. They now have their routine down to an art form. The rewards have been their sense of teamwork, more free time to enjoy together, and an increase in affection. Need we say more?

Some working couples agree to share housework more or less equally. Others budget money to hire someone to take over some of the household chores. Whatever your situation, we'd like to challenge you to adopt the Nike slogan, "Just do it!"

There is a radical difference between saying you care and showing that you care. Once in a while, surprise your partner by doing an extra chore quietly, lovingly, and graciously. "When you do something for someone else, don't call attention to yourself...or the God who made you won't be applauding" (Matthew 6:1–2, *The Message*).

Stop Resisting Each Other

There is nothing wrong with different ways of doing things, unless we decide to make them wrong. Have you ever noticed that men and women try to earn brownie points in different ways?

Men often think that they will get multiple points when they do something large and grandiose for their wives. Perhaps they take her on a fabulous vacation or they buy her a brand-new car. They assume that they score less when they do something small and less significant. They often have no idea that to many women, vacuuming is foreplay. Tucking the children into bed, helping with the little ones' homework, opening a door, arriving home for dinner on time, paying the bills, all get high marks in a woman's mind.

Most women give an equal score to big and little things. Every sacrifice for love gets noticed. If there are no little things being done by her husband, a woman feels unloved, because she has no tangible sign that he cares. Meanwhile her husband, who is focused on some big thing he can do for her, feels unloved and unappreciated when she asks for more.

At times it's easy for women to get into the habit of complaining about what their husbands don't do, while neglecting to acknowledge what they do do. Many women get irritated when they sense their husbands' need for affirmation. Perhaps this is because many women believe that housework is thankless work. They rarely, if ever, hear words of appreciation for their work coming from their husbands.

Human beings get upset when their contributions to the team aren't noticed and mentioned. Each partner needs to make a decision not only to be reliable and responsible, but also to champion the other.

A homemaker who had heard her husband complaining for

months about the children's toys cluttering their home, went out and bought some attractive shelves and bins. She worked on sorting, organizing, and eliminating. Her husband was surprised and thrilled. She said, "Don's face lit up like a Christmas tree."

When we do the little things that mean a lot, it is our way of saying, "I'm taking you seriously. I'm trying. I care about your comfort in our home and in our relationship."

Have you ever given your partner permission to speak up when he or she feels there isn't a mutual sharing of responsibility? Inbred in each one of us seems to be an overwhelming desire to be special, meaning that we desire our spouse to give a little more to us than we give back. It just doesn't seem natural to be an equally contributing mate.

And that's true; it isn't natural. It's supernatural. We follow the example of Jesus Christ, Lord of the universe, who stooped down to wash His disciples' dirty, dusty feet. Why? Because everyone else in that room thought it was someone else's job.

Decision #7
"I Will Be Responsible and Reliable"

For Reflection and Discussion

1. Who does what in your home? Initial the chores you take on as your responsibility.

   Taking out the trash
   Emptying all the wastebaskets
   Grocery shopping
   Preparing meals
   Clean up and dishes
   Laundry
   Mowing the lawn
   Taking garbage cans to the street and back
   Cleaning the bathrooms
   Cleaning the kitchen
   Vacuuming

Dusting
Cleaning the living and dining room
Caring for elderly parents
Balancing our checkbook
Writing checks and sending bills
Handling our investments
Decorating the house
Taking care of home repaires
Arranging our vacation
Planning our date night
Making reservations for dinner, buying movie tickets, etc.
Getting the baby-sitter
Giving gifts
Tending indoor plants
Straightening up the living areas
Doing annual spring cleaning
Sending out cards and letters
Cleaning the vehicles
Maintaining vehicles
Gardening
If you have children, add those responsibilities to your list.

2. What top five tasks could you take responsibility for and do to improve your marriage?

DECISION EIGHT

"I Will Be Honest"

John and Sally were enjoying the empty-nest stage of life. All of their children had graduated from college and were set up in their own places. Their youngest daughter, Sarah, was accustomed to being supported. All the way through college, John and Sally had paid off Sarah's significant credit card charges without confronting her spending habits.

Six months had passed since she began her new job. Sarah was continuing to live beyond her means and kept expecting that her parents would bail her out. John was adamant that this needed to stop. He and Sally agreed to cut the cash flow to their youngest. They informed Sarah of their decision.

A month later, Sarah got her mother away by herself. With tears streaming down her cheeks, she informed her mother of her latest financial crisis. There had been a party at work, and she needed to have the perfect outfit. Surely her mother could understand; her job depended on her making a good impression. When asked what she had charged, Sarah confessed to almost $500 in damages. Her mother was aghast. She knew that once again her daughter was in way over her head. Sally gave her the money and told her not to mention it to her dad.

Eventually John found out. He expressed shock on multiple levels. It was incomprehensible to him that Sally had gone behind his back and disregarded their agreement. He found it hard to believe that she was unwilling to allow Sarah to experience any logical consequences of her choices. He was angry that she had included their daughter in the lie.

After years of counseling, we believe that if couples are not committed to this core decision of honesty, the possibility of their experiencing a lifetime love affair is significantly diminished. Dishonesty acts as a virus in a marriage.

A marriage without truth is a marriage without passion. If that strikes you as an odd statement, think back to your dating days. As your future mate began to reveal himself or herself to you and trusted you with information not shared with anyone else, it was intoxicating. The act of being truthful became a point of passion.

Stating our truth is foundational to knowing who we are: discovering, defining, and owning ourselves. Receiving another's truth is a sacred trust, one of the highest ways of validating that person and his or her right to exist. Only when both spouses' truth is welcomed does a couple learn that their marriage is big enough for two. The true test of love is how we face the truth.

Marriages where truth isn't welcome are passionless prisons. Neither partner can be real; neither feels welcomed as an interesting, creative, whole person. Freedom is blocked. Friendship doesn't exist, and intimacy is absolutely impossible.

The decision to tell the truth sounds so easy, but how challenging it is. It is a two-pronged assignment. We have to learn to speak our truth, but we also have to welcome our partners' expression of truth, no matter how foreign or threatening it may seem to us. Cowards need not apply.

Psychologist Rollo May said, "The twentieth-century man has taken the fig leaf from the genitals and put it on his face." If you don't have a person with whom you can share your thoughts, feelings, needs, failure, and anger, you start to believe that you couldn't possibly be loveable. We all have a cruel internal judge who condemns us for having those thoughts, feelings, or needs. Our greatest fear is exposure. Over time our fig leaf becomes our reality. Hiding and fear go together.

Dave confesses: When I am afraid of my faults, I become defensive. I either accuse my wife or I excuse myself. When I am afraid of my feelings, I become distant. When I am afraid of losing my freedom, I become demanding.

We try to act the opposite of what we know is really true. We try to do better, to be more disciplined, to be more perfect. We become like lone rangers who depend only on themselves and their willpower. God wants us to be more honest and connected.

Dishonesty, whether in the form of pretending, withholding, or out-and-out lies, works against love. A relationship must be based on honesty if it is to flourish and grow. Intimacy is always arrived at through the tunnel of truth.

Trouble on Planet Earth

It's easy to tell ourselves that since we don't set out to deliberately deceive our partners, we are basically honest people. No doubt we are people of integrity on the big issues, but many times small lies of convenience can add up to a false picture. When this becomes our reality, the life and passion begins to seep out of our relationships.

Have you noticed that you can withhold your truth, yet not intentionally lie? Each of us can come up with multiple excuses to justify why we withhold our truth. We call these rationalizations. Perhaps we could term them "rational lies." Most of the time these rationalizations are made to protect us or to serve our own purposes.

Here are some of the occasions and reasons we use to justify dishonesty. Perhaps you can relate to some of them.

I want to avoid hurting my spouse's feelings. Some people are brutally truthful. There is a total absence of grace. There is a fine line between dishonesty and championing. In marriage the more mature we get, the more our critical spirit softens. Our suggestion is not to ask a question if you're not open to hearing an honest answer.

I don't want to disappoint my partner. Becky and Jim are building their dream house. Before the project began they sat down and worked out a budget. Now they are eight months into the project with Jim acting as the general contractor. In order to finish their home as they had dreamed, Jim will have to go over budget. Because he doesn't want to disappoint Becky and because he wants to appear competent and capable, he orders a new credit card and charges items on it. He withholds that particular truth from Becky, who now has no idea the financial pressure Jim is carrying.

I want to avoid conflict. Thom was delighted to get an invitation to a Super Bowl party from the guys at work. He needs an all-male day. He is also apprehensive, however. How will Ginger react? He puts off bringing it up until Friday evening of Super Bowl weekend. His wife is disappointed. She wanted him to spend the day with her. Ginger reminds him how little couple-time they've had in the last two weeks. He sighs, sucks it up, and says, "Okay, I'll watch the game with you on Sunday." She's happy, and he's left with a bad taste in his mouth. She has no idea how important this was to him and that he wasn't really being honest.

I'm afraid of being known. Gordon and Diane are in bed. She's feeling amorous, so she initiates some love play. He tenses up and turns away from her. The next day at work he is going to have a performance review. He's terrified of losing his job. After all, he is forty-five, and it seems as if everyone else in the company is under thirty-five. He hasn't the courage to share this with Diane, especially since she's expecting their third child. He doesn't want another child, but he's never told her that either. Diane feels his hesitancy, takes it personally, and falls asleep feeling rejected. Gordon is left staring at the ceiling wishing that he could talk with her.

I am afraid of being left. Frank comes up behind Joyce in the kitchen. He gives her a bear hug and tells her that he would enjoy making love. She's promised to complete a project for their daughter's high school, due the next morning. In addition, she's not feeling well. Their teenage kids are due back in thirty-five minutes, and she desperately wants to take a few quiet moments for herself before the evening onslaught hits. Instead of verbalizing any of her truth to Frank, she follows him into the bedroom. She is afraid that if she turns him down he could use it as an excuse to find someone else—that just happened to neighborhood couple.

She offers Frank her body but not her mind, her emotions, or her soul. She fantasizes about time alone while he's making love. She fakes an orgasm. She condemns him in her mind for wanting sex. She resents him intensely. Meanwhile Frank is completely in the dark. He has been disturbed recently by Joyce's lack of passion, but he's not sure he wants to know the truth, so he remains silent and never brings it up.

I want the upper hand in this marriage. Bob wants to have total control. Since his wife Darlene is a stay-at-home mother, she is completely dependent on him financially. He has banned her from visiting her parents or from having any of her friends over. When he leaves for work, he gives her a list of chores that need to be accomplished by the time he gets home. He phones her at various times during the day to make sure that she is really home. He makes her beg him for money.

Darlene does a little baby-sitting on the side. One day out of total frustration, she orders a credit card in her name. It seems to her that the only way to have any freedom is to deceive him. Over the next few months, she starts to use the credit card. For a while, she is able to keep up with the minimum payments out of her babysitting money, but it becomes increasingly difficult. The unpaid balance begins to increase.

I am embarrassed. Bonnie is exhausted. It has been a day that unraveled. She drops onto the couch in order to catch a thirty-minute nap while the baby sleeps. Neither of them wakes up. Two hours later she hears Marvin's car in the driveway. She panics. The house is a mess. Toys are everywhere, the lunch dishes are still in the sink, the laundry isn't folded. She can't bear his look of disapproval with the accompanying question, "What did you do all day?" Instead of telling him that she feels like a child caught by a disapproving parent, she starts making excuses. She fabricates a story about taking the baby to the doctor's office (which is true) and having to wait three hours (which isn't true).

I'm afraid of being seen as "bad" (or jealous, selfish, confused, cowardly, etc.). John and Kay have a beautiful son. Tyler is two years old and he has already undergone thirteen surgeries. He shouldn't have survived, but he has. Kay and John nicknamed Tyler "their million-dollar baby." Their medical bills are enormous and the pressure intense. At first John had barely warmed up to Tyler because he was so sure that this child would be taken from him by death. Kay had sensed his distance and had been tremendously hurt by it. She then distanced from John, and that distance has never been bridged.

In his heart, John has been wrestling with his faith. "Does God exist? Is He like a narcotic that I take when life seems too complicated? How can I say I have faith in God when I constantly wonder if He is really there? Why do others see answered prayers when I've been praying for two years and all I get are doctor bills?"

None of this struggle is verbalized or shared with anyone. Instead, John just feels a deep shame and continual condemnation.

He finds himself so alone and so empty, but he is afraid that if Kay knew all of his doubts and fears about connecting with God or their son Tyler, she might walk out on him.

I believe that submission means I must swallow my truth. Helen's husband is an angry man. He phones while away on a business trip and asks her to book some plane reservations for him at a specific time. When she phones back to let him know the only times available, she has to endure a verbal tirade about her incompetence and stupidity.

Helen once read a book full of rules about being a good Christian wife. She tries to follow the advice found on those pages. Once she went to meet him at the airport with nothing on under her coat. He laughed at her in an unkind way. Another evening, after she'd put the children down, she decided to surprise him and his business partners at the airport so they wouldn't have to hire a limo to get home. He was polite in front of his partners, but the moment they were alone he wanted to know what she was doing out that late at night.

Helen keeps creating a home for him, raising their children, carrying most of the responsibil-

notes

DOES THIS MAKE MY REAR END LOOK BIG?

ity in the marriage, believing in her heart of hearts that it is wrong biblically to speak up. Meanwhile, her husband gets increasingly angry, and she gets thinner.

Newlywed dishonesty

After we've said, "I do," we often find ourselves withholding our truth in order to protect our "us." Secretly, we are terrified that our "us" can't handle two individuals. If we love each other we believe we'll see eye-to-eye on most things. Often the new bride is invested in the marriage being a fairytale, so she accommodates herself to whatever her husband wants. She becomes his *Revised Standard Version*. In the process, she strangles the life out of herself and finds herself dissatisfied.

Her new groom may sense some of his bride's discontent, but he's not sure if he wants to raise the issue. He's afraid that she might confirm what he most fears. He already is feeling inadequate to the task of marriage—what if she isn't happy? His solution is to get lost in his work and to ride his bike three hours a day. If he's unusually honest with himself, he might have to admit that it is not so bad getting things his way.

Often newlyweds are so concerned about pleasing each other that neither one gets what he or she wants. We may push the uncomfortable feelings of discontent under the carpet because we don't want to rock the boat, and yet we begin to feel a discomfort that maybe we can't be ourselves in this relationship.

When Truth Isn't Spoken

Under the guise of protecting a spouse or of labeling ourselves as optimists, we sometimes keep the peace and tell ourselves that this really isn't a good time to bring up our truth. Other times when we don't speak up, and don't give ourselves permission to be heard, it is a self-esteem issue. We don't value our own truth as much as we value our spouses' right to theirs.

Paul, in his letter to the Ephesian church, challenges us to "speak the truth in love." In the *Living Bible* paraphrase, we are challenged to be different from dependent children who swallow every lie we hear." Instead, we will lovingly follow the truth at all times—speaking truly, dealing truly, living truly, and so become more and more in every way like Christ who is the Head of His body, the church" (Ephesians 4:15, TLB).

Speaking your truth can be challenging, especially when you are concerned about your spouse's ability to hear a truth different from his or her own. When your truth isn't received with open arms, you are left unsettled. When your truth is discovered, you are threatened. When it is attacked, you are intimidated and resentful. When it is rejected, you are minimized.

Truth doesn't cause the problem; our response to the truth sometimes does. As one man put it, "The day I heard you say 'no' was the day I started fantasizing about someone who would always say 'yes'."

When Truth Isn't Heard

We fake orgasms. We swallow our true feelings. We hide our disappointments, hurts, failures, and needs. We disown our desires, likes, and dislikes. We find it incredibly hard to find any common ground. We shut ourselves down. We live a lie.

Then we wake up one morning with the realization that we've stopped talking about the really important things. Our unspoken truths cling like burrs to clothing. We stay in this shut-off mode for a while, and then we may courageously try again. If we find our truth laughed at, attacked, rebuffed, or rejected and our honesty punished, we may shut down completely.

It's easy at that point to believe that your spouse doesn't understand you, without owning your part in the crumbling integrity of your marriage. Oh, you may be polite, but you're almost dead. You search for other confidantes, healthy and unhealthy. You may even search the Internet for someone who will always say "yes." The distance and silence between you and your partner becomes tangible. You aren't inside each other's hearts. You've learned that sharing your truth with your partner leads to disaster, and frankly you wish your mate had remained silent. A cynicism seeps into your spirit.

Solomon writes in the Book of Proverbs, "The tongue that brings healing is a tree of life, but a deceitful tongue crushes the spirit" (15:4). If honesty is not welcomed into a marriage, partners turn into inmates locked together by a vow. Their spirits are crushed. They are estranged from each other, and find themselves invested in maintaining the maximum distance from one another in order to prevent hostilities from erupting.

Honesty makes a connection real. If deception comes through the door, intimacy goes out the same door. Deception undermines a couple's "us." No longer is their relationship founded on reality and trust. It undermines the depth of their knowledge of each other. It undermines their connection. It denies any problem, so they don't mature into problem solvers. It destabilizes their relationship, makes resolve impossible, and leaves them feeling hopeless.

Very few, if any, of us, would be willing to give our partners the authority to lie to us whenever they think it is for our good. In what an immature, dependent, childlike place that decision would put us. And in what an evil place that decision would put our partners.

Every time we are dishonest, it leaves a scar on our character and sets a precedent in our marriage. Whenever a lie is uncovered, trust is eroded. You will no longer see your spouse in the same way again. The longer one continues to be dishonest, the lower the chances are of rebuilding trust.

If we can't trust each other, everything else collapses. Problems become less tolerable, compromises less appealing, and honest connection impossible. Intimacy is a thing of the past. Our relationship is undermined. Mutual honesty, on the other hand, reinforces the foundation of a marriage.

Can I Speak the Truth?

"Therefore each of you must put off falsehood and speak truthfully to his neighbor, for we are all members of one body." (Ephesians 4:25) As we have discovered, we can offer multiple justifications for not speaking our truth. Sometimes we don't know what our truth is. Other times, we question our truth's value to our partners. Other times we're afraid of the reaction we will get. Sometimes we don't really want anything to change.

There is no question that the true test of honesty comes when there may be a cost to telling the truth. If you want to be a person of integrity, you need to pay the price: be straightforward, honest, and upfront with God, yourself, and your spouse.

If you don't want to feel like a phony, if you want to feel less resentful, if you want change, and if you want to be an equal contributing partner, your truth needs to be told. If in your marriage you haven't allowed yourself a voice, you may not know where you stand with regard to some issues. It is our suggestion that you journal. Write out your thoughts and feelings. Try to describe your position. If you are unable to articulate it clearly, do some research, ask questions, seek the perspective of others, pray, and then try again to put your perspective on paper. Do that until you have clarity. Then set up an appointment with your husband or wife. Share your truth and the process that you went through to come to your truth. Ask your spouse to listen, using the suggestions found in the next section.

Can I Hear Truth?

If you are trying to get a friend's puppy to eat something out of your hand, what do you do when the puppy comes near? Do you wait patiently and encourage him, or do you lunge at him? Obviously, it would be unwise to lunge. You'd scare him off.

In no way are we insinuating that spouses are like dogs, but there is a principle here that applies. When your partner dares to come close with a truth that makes you feel anxious or uncomfortable in some way, do you lunge? Do you attack, judge, preach, interrogate, or distance yourself? Do you collapse, seek revenge, or defensively send out a decoy? Do you blow like a stick of dynamite? If you, in some way, make your partner feel bad for speaking honestly, is it any wonder that he or she is hesitant to open up in the marriage? Remember, honesty must never be punished.

What is it that you need to do differently? What is it that you would like your spouse to do differently?

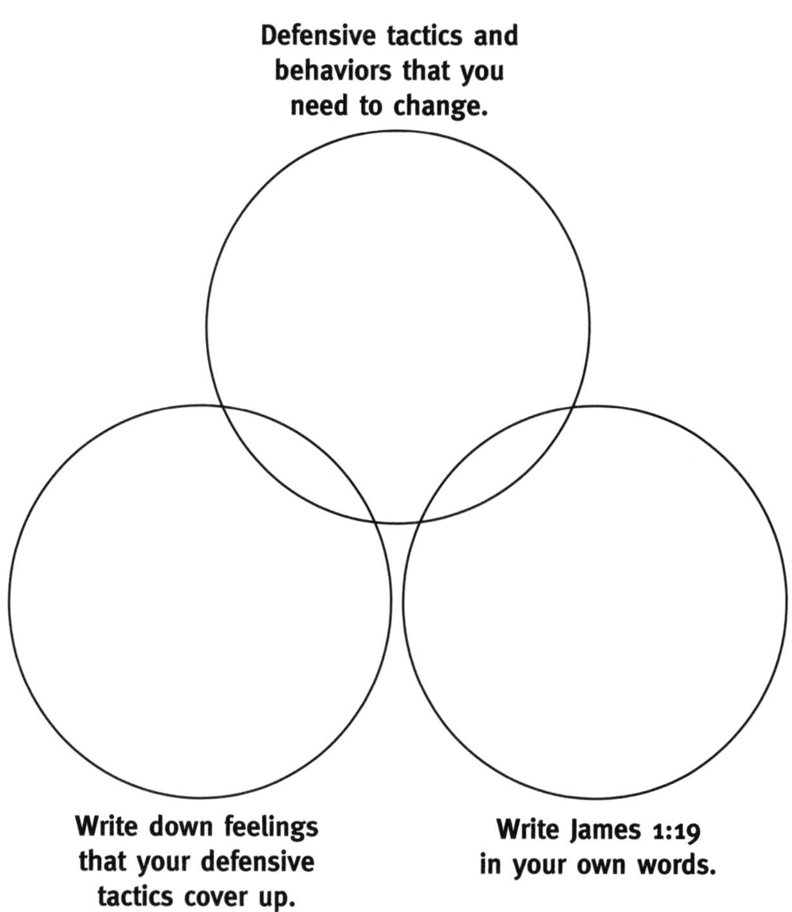

If you reject each other's truth, your marriage no longer feels safe. **Listening to your partner is not the same as surrendering to his or her opinion.** It's once again acknowledging that your marriage is big enough for two imperfect human beings. The challenge is to hear without capitulating, rebelling, or attacking.

We need to learn to hold our partners' truth in our hands, to consider it, to pray over it, and to value it as their truth. We need to allow them to influence us.

James challenges us, "My dear brothers, take note of this: Everyone should be quick to listen, slow to speak and slow to become angry" (1:19). Nothing about James' challenge is easy. Most of us, if we do what comes naturally, are quick to become angry, quick to speak, and slow to listen. There is another option. Defensiveness can be replaced by support, concern, and curiosity.

If you struggle with hearing each other's truth, you might find it helpful to find a place free of interruptions. Decide who will be the first speaker. Use a timer so that the truth being shared is restricted to five minutes. The listener is to encourage the other with his or her eyes and body language. If necessary, periodically ask, "Is there more?" If a question arises in the listener's mind, write it down. Refrain from asking your questions until after your partner has had his or her full time to talk.

If it is necessary to ask a question, remember that good questions seek to understand the feelings and motivations of the other person. Questions aren't about the listener; they are about the truth-teller. "Can you help me understand why you are hesitant to buy this house?" is a much better question than "I don't believe that you think that I will help bring in money to pay for the house, is that right?"—a barely concealed attack disguised in question form.

Listen for understanding. Remember that agreement is not a prerequisite for listening. After the listener has a grasp of what the other person is attempting to share, the listener can summarize the other's perspective. Discover if you missed it or truly understood your mate's perspective.

Now it is the listener's turn to be the speaker. The same suggestions apply. Promise that you will no longer punish honesty. Remember, you're not doing something that comes naturally. If you are successful, honesty has been received in an atmosphere of grace into your marriage.

I promise you, my partner, a person—
Not a puppet, a person—
Growing in an understanding of who he is because of
whose he is.
I am a child of the Almighty God with gifts, talents, dreams,
hopes, opinions, interests, thoughts, and perspectives.
I am unfinished, imperfect, and at times sinful.
I will let you down,
But I will also hold you up.
There will be times my truth will hurt you
But I will promise not to deliver it in a hurtful way.
To do less than share my truth would diminish me as a person.
At the same time I will see you as a person
Growing in your understanding of who you are.
I will see you as a unique child of the Almighty God
With gifts, talents, dreams, hopes, opinions,
Interests, thoughts, and perspectives.
You are unfinished, imperfect, and, at times, sinful.
You will let me down
But you will also hold me up.
There will be times that your truth will hurt me
Even so I want to hear it.
I don't want you to feel diminished as a person.
You are a person. I am a person.
I promise you a person.

What Do I Do with the Big Secrets?

Often from the beginning of a marriage, when faced with the choice to share or withhold truth, some people opt for a vast accumulation of untruths, big and small. When one mate is chronically deceptive, the lies build until they overtake the person and the marriage. They can't be ignored anymore. We hear of money issues, secret accounts, unrevealed debt, failure to pay taxes, a second family, children from a previous marriage or relationship, or a criminal record. The trust is devastated in these marriages. Often smaller lies are necessary to maintain the big lie.

One man lost a significant amount of money in the stock market. He was too embarrassed to tell his wife, especially since she had warned him against it in the first place. When she wanted to know the status of his investments, he told her that the statements weren't in and he'd follow up on it. The web thickened.

Infidelity tops the painful list of big lies. There are different types and degrees of infidelity; a one-time, one-night stand affects a marriage deeply, but the effect is quite different from that of an ongoing, clandestine affair. Often affairs involve far more than one lie.

Deciding to bring these untruths out in the open is like bringing sticks of dynamite to the center of your home and setting them off. The complexity of telling the truth is enormous, but a secret not told is like a wrecking ball hanging over the marriage, ready to strike at any time.

If you find yourself carrying a big lie around we would like to suggest that:

1. You write your confession in a letter. Admit the ambivalence you feel and why you have not told the truth up to this time. Then go to bed.
2. Find someone to share this letter with—a pastor or a Christian therapist would be our suggestion.
3. Work with that person on what the next step should be.

Decision #8
"I Will Be Honest"

For Reflection and Discussion

1. Here is a partial list of rationalizations for dishonesty in a marriage. Check any of the excuses that you have used in the past to justify withholding your truth.

___I want to avoid hurting my spouse's feelings.
___I want to avoid disappointing my spouse.
___I want to look good.
___I want to avoid conflict.
___I'm afraid of being known.
___I'm afraid my spouse will sense my insecurity.
___It's easier.
___I'm afraid that my spouse would leave if he or she really knew me.
___I want my way.
___I want the upper hand in this marriage.
___I was embarrassed.
___I'm afraid of being seen as "bad" (or jealous, selfish, confused, cowardly, etc.).
___I believe that submission requires me to swallow my truth.
___I'm afraid to own my own truth.
___I don't want to threaten the status quo.
___I want to protect our "us."

DECISION NINE

"I Will Connect with You"

With stars in their eyes, Julie and Randall told us how they sat on Julie's front porch talking for hours the first night they met. That night they discovered they felt exactly the same way about everything—movies, families, responsibility, and faith. She didn't want to go inside. He didn't want to go home. So they sat on the porch talking together all night.

Then life happened. They kept expecting things to return to normal, but they never did. At our house, we call this stage "new normal."

Add two jobs, a few years, a couple of kids, and we can hardly find the time to go to the bathroom, let alone have an intimate discussion into the wee hours of the morning. Does this dialogue resemble your reality?

Husband: Tell me about your day.

Wife: Don't ask. My entire day . . .

Child #1: Mommy, Mommy, Mommy, Mommy, MOMMY!

Husband: What about your day?

Child #2: (Shrieks)

Wife: Did you hit your baby brother? Did you?

Child #1: He made a face at me.

Wife: We don't hit each other in this family. I want you to sit in your room and think about yourself.

Child #1: (Tears and protests)

Husband: So what about your day?

Wife: Before I forget, we're out of milk. I've got to make a note of that.

Sound familiar? Even if you don't have kids, the typical evening can be characterized by stress, distractions, late hours at work, and separate to-do lists. Time to connect seems like a distant memory.

Before marriage your biggest decisions are what to do on Saturday evening, who will be in your wedding party, and where you will spend your honeymoon. After the wedding, you deal with the nitty-gritty of finances, home location, job realities, sexual adjustments, and children—just to mention a few things. The tendency of many couples is to let the whining of the baby, the barking of the dog, the needs of the kids, the pressures of work, and the interference of the phone keep them from letting each other into their separate worlds.

More often than we care to enumerate, we run into couples that just take turns talking; they rarely, if ever, connect. Parallel play is normal for two- and three-year-olds; children often use the same sandbox and even the same toys, but they are playing alone next to each other, not with each other. It's not a good idea for adults . . . yet many couples live this way, only connecting around common activities.

Jan's memory: We knew we were in trouble when our son was three years old. Dave and I were in the car alone for some reason. I pointed toward the sky and said, "Look, honey, a helicopter." I was stunned that those words had come out of my mouth. I burst out laughing. Obviously, it had been too long since we'd been out together alone. Most of my conversation was focused on three-year-olds. That day we made a commitment to have regular childless moments—date times, where we could communicate at an adult level.

What about you? When you and your spouse are together, what do you talk about?

Hiding Takes One

Adam and Eve had a unique, unbroken connection with their Creator. He walked and talked with them on a regular basis. Can you comprehend what it might be like to stroll with God?

notes

The relational God, the personal God who affects us and is affected by us, created Adam, Eve, and each of us with an innate need for connection with Himself and with other people. In fact, the only "not good" God uttered during the process of creation was his acknowledgement that Adam had no one of his kind with whom he could relate. So God created a woman, also made in the image of God, as a companion, confidante, and colaborer with her husband.

Isolation and detachment were not God's plan for mankind. He created everything for Adam and Eve's enjoyment, with one exception. God limited the two of them with these words: "You are free to eat from any tree in the garden; but you must not eat from the tree of the knowledge of good and evil, for when you eat it you will surely die" (Genesis 2:16,17).

These two human beings rebelled against God's structure. Anyway, what did "die" mean? They had no concept of death. They were surrounded by light, love, and security. You are no doubt familiar with the rest of the story. Since Adam and Eve chose to override God's plan, they opened themselves up to evil as well as good. They felt immediate separation from God. God didn't withdraw from them. Instead, they withdrew from Him.

God sought them out and initiated connection. "Then the eyes of both of them were opened, and they realized they were naked; so they sewed fig leaves together and made coverings for themselves. Then the man and his wife heard the sound of the Lord God as he was walking in the garden in the cool of the day, and they hid from the Lord God among the trees of the garden. But the Lord God called to the man, 'Where are you?' He answered, 'I heard you in the garden, and I was afraid because I was naked; so I hid' " (Genesis 3:7-10).

Adam and Eve's independent willfulness opened them up to evil, fear, and death. Nakedness, openness, and vulnerability were immediately terrifying. They covered their genitals, they withdrew from connection, they misperceived God, they blamed each other, and they trusted no one.

God didn't intend hiding to be a part of their lives or ours, but we humans have been hiding from love ever since. We may even have created an equation in our heart where: revealing ourselves = pain. Sometimes we devalue the capacity of God and spouse to love us or to be there for us. In that way we hide from our need, our dependency. Then we're in control but not connected. Other times we hide from our truth. We try to whitewash what is going on inside us, and we attempt to keep everyone in our world happy. It takes only one person in a marriage taking an antilove stance to limit the possibility of intimacy.

God doesn't want hiding to be a part of our lives. Through Solomon's writing, God lets us know that lack of connection is depressing and cold. "But woe to the one who falls when there is not another to lift him up. Furthermore, if two lie down together, they keep warm, but how can one be warm alone?" (Ecclesiastes 4:10,11, NASB).

God knows that isolation is hell. Without connection there is no grace, safety, or warmth. The God who takes delight in His people (Psalm 149:4), the God whose character is love, the God who does not withdraw His love from us, came up with a relational plan to make it possible for willful, limit hating, fearful humans to be back in connection with Him. He communicated in a way humans could understand. He subjected Himself to the limits of time and space. He became a relational human being, Jesus Christ.

Intimacy Takes Two

Only when you commit to a lifelong love affair with your husband or wife is your capacity for intimacy put to the test.

Jody kept trying to draw Kyle into their marriage. She'd suggest ideas for weekend trips they could do together. He'd listen, and yet when Jody asked him to commit to an activity or a weekend, he'd say that he didn't know. When she raised an issue that caused her concern, his reply was often "whatever." If she shared a frustration from her work, Kyle would suggest that she quit. Then he would walk away.

Jody suggested that she'd enjoy more affection and physical intimacy. He took it as a criticism and came back with a zinger about how she wasn't so hot in bed either. When at home, Kyle spent his time glued to the TV or working on the computer.

Jody grieved her husband's refusal to connect. She kept extending suggestions and options for the two of them. When those were consistently rebuffed, she told Kyle that her first choice would be to do things with him. If he wasn't interested or wouldn't commit, she would start planning more activities with her girlfriends.

Jody's hopes of deep connection with her husband were dashed. She discovered that marriage can be the loneliest place on earth unless both partners are intentional about their connection. If we are not intentional, there is no possibility of having a relationship.

Allowing yourself to be known is a lifelong challenge. If both of you committed to be mates for a lifetime, it is cruel and unnecessary punishment for one of you to be a lifeless, hidden mate.

Growth, intimacy, and maturity are not the result of being nice to each other for fifty years. A connection is created by commitment, honesty, and a willingness to grow and change on the part of both partners.

Making Connection a Priority

Two distinctly unique people create a marriage. Each new day, you must let your spouse know who you are, and you must learn to love the person he or she is. If you are both intentional about it, your mutual connection relieves some of your loneliness. Together you will experience what God intended when He said, "It is not good for the man to be alone . . ." (Genesis 2:18).

When we don't grab and schedule connection time, then we start to feel like robots. We may accomplish multiple tasks, but it's as if the heart has gone out of us.

We asked some couples who are intentional about their connection how they do it. We pass on some of their ideas to you.

Greeting ritual. Russ and Patty concentrate on making the first five minutes of their morning and the first five minutes when they are reunited at the end of the day a pleasant time of verbal communication, eye contact, and warm affection.

The pause that refreshes. Damien and Amy have a treasured ritual most evenings. Damien brings a cup of hot tea to Amy after dinner. They go into the family room and sit together. Their children know not to interrupt, short of the house burning down. This is the time that they share their day with each other.

Pillow talk. Having a relaxing conversation with each other is one of the best ways to end your day. Dale put it this way: "The best part of my marriage is talking about the day's events in bed each night and then holding each other until we fall asleep."

Jim and Shirley use pillow time to confess ways that they hurt each other during the day. They ask for forgiveness and then pray together. They say that this connection time has revolutionized their marriage. Now when they are tempted to let a barb out during the day, they bite their tongue because they know they'll only have to confess it later that night.

Ralph and Penny do a word completion exercise as they lie together in bed. "This (action or word) really helped me feel connected to you today." Or, "This (action or word) resulted in my feeling disconnected."

Weekly issue time. We each get one hour a week to bring up issues that are causing us concern. We schedule them onto our calendar on different days. We did this to keep our problem discussion from polluting every day of the week. It also helps us know that our issues are important in our marriage. Obviously, if an emergency issue raises its head, we are free to raise it whether it's our scheduled time or not.

Hug time. Tara and Shane made a pact that if one of them approached the other with a hug, the other one had to hug back for a one-minute minimum. Tara said that she had to ask Shane to develop a sense of timing. If she was busy pulling something out of the oven, or running late for an appointment, it would become a five-second hug and the one-minute hug would happen later.

Travel time. Sometimes we read to each other and then discuss what we are reading. Other times we listen to a tape and interact about that. Sometimes we just gab. Sometimes we delight in music together.

Mealtimes. Come prepared to share something interesting.

Intimacy via long distance. Bill and Lois, who both have to travel for work, tell us that they are separated Monday through Friday most weeks. They both enjoy a certain TV show. From their hotel rooms they phone each other a few moments before the show. They watch it separately, but together, and laugh and carry on. They tell us that hearing each other laugh brings joy to their hearts. It makes them feel connected.

Cheryl and Aaron, who are engaged, are separated by 300 miles, yet they play Monopoly together over the phone once a week.

Too tired for love? A young married couple, Ray and Anne, were less than satisfied with their time for sexual intimacy. They had twins, and Anne felt as though she ran nonstop until she hit the bed at night. Some nights it seemed that she was asleep the second she hit the pillow. Both of them wanted to make love when they had more to give, so they set their alarm for one hour before the twins awoke. They became early morning lovers. Ray said that he went to work with a smile on his face on those days.

Date time. Alternate the planning. Read the LifeMates book *Dates for Mates* by Lisa Keyes and Debbie Black. One couple told us that they celebrate the day of their first kiss together every month. The husband is in charge of planning their adventures for the evening or day.

Prayer time together. John and Marion create a prayer list together. They then divide it up according to the days of the week. In the evening, before going to bed, they hold hands and pray through their daily list together. They tell us that they treasure this time of connection.

Encourage and nurture your spiritual life by worshipping together, meditating together, attending spiritual retreats together, and reading and discussing spiritual books.

Once-a-year intimacy marathon. Nathaniel and his wife started the tradition of a twenty-four-hour intimacy marathon. There are no children, no TV, no books, no newspapers, no phones, and no disturbances. Only personal issues can be discussed. They use a portion of their time to set goals for their marriage and their family.

Running errands together. Another twosome finds couple time by running errands together on Saturday morning. It would be more efficient if he and she did the errands separately, but that is not the point. Marital rituals don't have to be efficient.

Physical intimacy. We suggest that you schedule at least one time a week. If there are young children in your home, our suggestion is that the husband get them to bed and give his wife an hour to unwind before they talk and make love.

These ideas are just a beginning. You might meet for lunch once a week, take a class together, select a hobby or project you would both enjoy, read jokes to each other, read a book together, create a new tradition together. The point is to be intentional about connecting. Take the time to talk to your partner about other ideas that you might have. Remember, we each say "I do" one day at a time.

Sometimes when your spouse approaches you for connection time, your anxiety increases. Somehow communicating has taken on serious, somber, and negative overtones. That's why each marriage needs a balance between "head talk" and "heart talk."

Head Talk and Heart Talk

"Head talk" is just the day-to-day sharing of reality. It is lighthearted, less intense interaction. Head-talk conversations aren't earth shattering, just interesting. What's happening with your favorite team, something cute that one of the kids did or said, a new restaurant you would like to visit, a joke you heard at work, something you read in the newspaper or something your neighbor said.

"Heart talk" consists of a more intimate exchange between spouses. We're not only sharing facts and events, we are sharing ourselves. Therefore, we talk about our needs and desires, our feelings, fears, and uncertainties, our history and our hopes and dreams. In heart-talk moments we let our partners know how their actions have impacted us. We clarify our limits and confess our faults and our mistakes to each other.

Heart talk is a sacred trust. Once this becomes a part of your marriage, you need to commit to confidentiality. Nothing your spouse reveals can be shared with anyone else. It can't be used as exhibit A in the next argument. It is to be treasured and held in your heart.

One woman put a Band-Aid on her forehead as a signal that she was hurting and wanted some heart talk time. One day she and her husband came home to find their five-year-old daughter with a Band-Aid on her forehead. When they asked what had happened, she said she needed "Mommy and Daddy talk time." Another couple created a wooden heart-shaped magnet, which they put on the refrigerator. Either of them can take the magnet off the fridge and bring it to the partner.

We personally have discovered that our heart-talk times are more successful if they don't happen when we're hungry, when we're tired after ten o'clock in the evening, when the children need attention, or in the middle of a televised sports event.

We would like to issue a foundational warning. We need to talk in such a way that our mates will be able to listen to us. Here are several suggestions.

- Guard the amount of complaining that you do.
- Guard the length of your monologues. Keep them short.
- Guard against negative judgments that your spouse doesn't also share.
- Guard against being too predictable in the following ways: talking only about yourself, talking about the same topics continually, holding to the same opinions, saying the same old thing.
- Guard against assuming that there is nothing more to discover. Ask questions for the purpose of understanding.

Every marriage needs to balance head talk and heart talk. If you expect every interaction to be heart talk, your mate won't want to come home for fear of what heavy topic you're going to hit him or her with tonight. If, on the other hand, all your communication is head talk, often one of you will be dissatisfied by the superficiality of your exchanges, longing for a deeper level of connection.

Revealing yourself to your partner has just begun! Never assume that you know everything there is to know about that interesting person you married.

Decision #9
"I Will Connect with You"

For Reflection and Discussion

1. "When we find ourselves alone together, we end up talking about . . ." Check the following topics that apply to your communication:

Other people
Our feelings
Our children
TV or movies
Work
Extended family issues
Problems that need to be solved
Hobbies
Tasks that need to be done
Upcoming vacations
Sports
Criticisms
Something we've learned
Gossip
Hopes and dreams
Our limits
Our relationship

Our understanding of ourselves
Our spiritual journey
Books we've read
Funny experiences
Finances
Physical exhaustion
Stress
Church activities
Distribution of chores
Politics
House decorations
Future purchases

What did you just learn about your connection time? Do you reveal yourselves intimately to each other when you talk? Is there anything you would like to change about your conversations?

2. Do you tell your spouse only the good things, the positives, and the successes? Do you keep the losses, the failures, the embarrassments, and any negatives hidden? Are you able to share all facets of your life with each other except asking for support and comfort? When your spouse raises a feeling, does your anxiety increase?

3. Listed below are some sentence completions. Use these to get to know each other in a different way. Enjoy this head-talk time together.

When I was growing up, my best friends were . .
What I liked about them was . . .
One of my favorite childhood memories is . . .
What I like best about being an adult is . . .
My favorite color is . . .
The last really great book I read was . . .
Three people in history I would most like to invite to dinner are . . . Why?
My best friend today, besides you, is . . . This is what

I enjoy about him (or her) . . .
One of my favorite Bible passages is . . .
I like these things about how I spend my day . . .
I would like these things to be different about my work/career in the next five years . . .
One of my fondest memories from our courtship is . . .
My taste in music seems to be . . .
One of my favorite songs is . . . Why?
Animals and I are . . .
If I could choose anyone to be a personal mentor it would be . . . Why?
One of my all-time favorite movies is . . . Why?
A four-week, all-expense paid trip I would like to take anywhere in the world is . . . Why?
You have influenced me most in this way . . .
One of the things I value most about our relationship is . . .
The five greatest achievements of my life are . . .

What is it that you need to do differently? What is it that you would like your spouse to do differently?

DECISION TEN

"I Will Reveal Myself to You"

When a relationship is new, two people love to share stories with each other. In a marriage, heart-talk times happen when the partners continue that tradition. You tell your own story to your spouse, he or she receives it and reciprocates. Revealing yourselves to each other can be done in many different ways. It begins when you seek to share what you know of yourselves with each other. Therefore the first step one needs to take is toward self-understanding.

Few, if any, of us enter marriage really knowing ourselves. As we rub up against each other each day of our life, we start to discover different facets of ourselves. As a result of living with another person who does things differently, we may begin to question the family pattern we were raised with. Do we want the way it was done in our home to dominate our present and future?

I must seek to know myself.

Gail was raised by parents who were warm one moment and distant and withdrawn the next. She was never able to pinpoint exactly why they switched. All she knew was that she'd have to pay penance indefinitely until suddenly, miraculously, they'd decide that she was the apple of their eye again.

During one of the times that she was deemed unworthy of their affection, she wrote in her diary about how unfair it all felt. Later that week, her mother found her locked diary, opened it, and read it. She punished her daughter severely based on what she read and pulled away from Gail emotionally for six days, acting the entire time as if her daughter had victimized her.

If Gail were asked about her parents' relationship, she'd have to admit that it was less than satisfying. She didn't question whether her folks loved each other. They seemed to, but she had to admit that Mom ran the show. In order not to be emotionally or physically cut off, Dad acquiesced on virtually everything. In fact, she remembered seeking out her father's perspective on issues only to be told, "This is what your mother thinks."

Gail's relationship to Bob, her husband, was an emotional roller coaster until Bob challenged her to journal her pattern of connection with him. Because she deeply loved Bob and because she was committed to personal growth, she followed his suggestion. What she discovered was that she would pull away emotionally whenever she felt disappointed or let down. They could go months without any physical intimacy as a result of her feathers being ruffled. If she sensed that Bob was looking in the direction of another woman she would treat the incident as if it were a full-fledged affair. She would accuse him of not really loving her and wanting to be with someone else.

> "Failure is the path of least persistence."

As a result of her willingness to stand back and see herself through her husband's eyes, Gail discovered that her choices in the present hurt her husband in much the same way that she had been hurt by her family's pattern in the past.

As a result of our families' comfort or discomfort with connection, we learn how to be in relationship. Acknowledging your family's impact is important to your marriage. Perhaps you no longer want your pattern to be what your family modeled.

We all tell stories with our lives. If you think you have no story to tell, perhaps you need to ask your spouse what your tendencies reveal about you. How does your partner think your past has influenced the way you are today?

Revealing Ourselves

There is a depth of intimacy that comes from sharing your experience of life with the person you love. But as you share your stories with each other, it is important that you make the following commitments.

I will talk openly and clearly with you.

Christie was out for dinner one evening with her fiancé, Gordon. As she looked around the restaurant, she became painfully aware of how many married couples were not conversing with each other. They'd greet the waiter with warmth and then avoid each other's eyes and stare at their food. It was as if there was an invisible wall between them.

That night Christie and Gordon made a pledge to keep communicating. They promised each other the unabridged version of who they were. They promised to keep their stories fresh, current, and coming. They couldn't help but wonder what had happened in the lives of the other couples in the restaurant. Had someone swallowed his words one too many times? Perhaps one or both of them didn't welcome the other's truth. Christie and Gordon left the restaurant determined to continually discover the partner each was choosing to spend a lifetime with.

Some couples talk, but in the process they sugarcoat and camouflage the truth so that it is unrecognizable.

A woman who was fascinated by genealogy hired an author to record her family history. In the process of researching her background, she discovered that her grandfather had been electrocuted in prison. She wanted to make this fact acceptable to those reading the genealogy. The author solved her dilemma. When the book came out it read, "One of her grandfathers occupied the chair of applied electricity in one of America's best known institutions. He was very much attached to his position and literally died in the harness."[1]

Don't make your spouse work as hard to decipher your words as did readers of this genealogy book! We would be wise to heed Solomon's warning: "Someone who holds back the truth causes trouble" (Proverbs 10:10, GNB).

I will admitting my feelings and fears.

One day a heartbroken woman sat in Dave's office and said, "I never know what he is thinking. I feel left out of his life." Her husband was afraid that she would leave him when she saw how insecure he was feeling, so he didn't open up to her. The sad fact was that because she didn't know what he was thinking, she was questioning whether he even loved her.

Another level of revealing ourselves to each other happens when we share our feelings.

Debbie had been so disappointed by the evening. She had spent the entire week preparing for their seventeen-year-old daughter's boyfriend to come for dinner. This was the first time that her daughter had expressed a desire to have her friend do something with the family. Debbie sensed that in her daughter's eyes he was more than a friend.

Debbie talked to Steve about how important this evening was. She asked him to make an effort to be home by six o'clock. Then she enlisted the help of their other child, Blaine, who was nine and who thought all girls, including his sister, had cooties. Blaine kept singing, "Sissy's got a boyfriend, yuck!"

Finally, in spite of her helper, everything was ready. The table looked beautiful, and the smells wafting from the oven were intoxicating. Debbie had let their daughter choose the menu. The doorbell rang. It was the honored guest, Jason. He was on time; now where was Steve? Late. Steve arrived home at seven o'clock, obviously in a grumpy frame of mind. He politely greeted everyone, made no comment as to why he was delayed, and then plunked himself down at the table. He didn't say two words the rest of the evening.

Debbie was upset. Not only was serving dinner delayed, which caused the meat to dry out, but she sensed her daughter's disappointment and felt as if she had had to carry the entire evening by herself. What was she going to do? If she shared her disappointment with Steve, she knew there was a good chance she might be misunderstood, he might be hurt, or it might start a conflict and spoil an otherwise pleasant day. But if she didn't share her feelings, what was she going to do with those feelings raging inside of her?

I will remember the importance of timing.

It is bad advice to tell couples that they must be honest and open about their feelings all the time. Healthy marriage partners reveal their feelings to each other, but not every second of every day. They choose their moments. Sometimes they choose not to immediately disclose their feelings.

Have you noticed that each of us, regardless of our feelings, has a choice of how we act in any given situation? There are many mornings that we don't feel like getting up, but we choose to. We might not feel like paying taxes, but we do it anyway. In life, we often feel one way and choose to act another. Feelings don't cause actions.

Some couples believe that when they feel anger, they immediately need to act on it. Consider stopping, taking a few breaths, and then deciding how and when to get your point across. Perhaps it would be wise to wait until you have further clarity. Perhaps you should wait until you have written down your feelings or talked to a counselor about the issue. Delaying often gives us time to develop an effective plan to achieve our goal. Teeth marks on our tongue can be, at times, a very wise choice. James cautions us to be "quick to listen, slow to speak and slow to become angry" (1:19).

There are times that our restraint will lead us to the awareness that we originally overreacted. At those moments we need to let some things run off our backs. We need to choose our battles rather than having an overreaction to every upsetting circumstance. (Obviously if your tendency is the opposite, and you swallow your feelings constantly, growth for you will involve speaking up about the feelings you have.) David and Amy Olsen, researchers who drew from a pool of 21,510 married couples in fifty states, discovered that eighty-two percent of these couples wished their spouses would be more expressive of their feelings.[2]

I will take the risk of disclosure.

There is definitely a risk involved when a marriage welcomes the feelings of each partner. Jesus is the only one who makes it 100 percent safe to bring our feelings, comfortable and uncomfortable, to Him. Husbands and wives are not so predictable. We all are imperfect, unpredictable, free, intelligent, emotional human beings, sometimes cooperative and sometimes resistant. But it is worth the risk.

Let's not pretend. Instead, using "I" statements, let's communicate our truth. The mistake that most of us make is to say, "I feel that you. . . ." That is not a feeling, and it is not an "I" statement. It is a judgment. No one wants to hear condemnation.

The expression of feeling is the beginning of healing, but judgments, accusations, characterizations, and problem solving are not feelings. For example: "If you really cared about me, you would have come home from work early" (judgment). "You're such an inconsiderate person" (accusation). "The answer is for you to leave work fifteen minutes earlier" (problem solving).

Instead say, "I feel . . . " and then add a feeling word. Often we find it awkward to find the word that best describes our internal state. Following is a list for your use of some of the most familiar feeling words.

Love: affectionate, caring, close, proud, passionate
Anger: frustrated, exasperated, enraged, indignant
Hurt: let down, disappointed, needy
Shame: embarrassed, guilty, regretful, humiliated, self-loathing
Fear: anxious, terrified, worried, obsessed, suspicious
Self-doubt: inadequate, unworthy, inept, unmotivated
Joy: happy, enthusiastic, full, elated, content
Sadness: depressed, melancholy, grief, anguish
Jealous: envious, selfish, yearning
Gratitude: appreciative, thankful, relieved, admiring
Lonely: desolate, abandoned, empty, rejected, longing.

I will share my ambivalent feelings.

Even when we try to stick with our own feelings ("I am feeling affectionate"), we often end up uncertain and confused about what is happening inside us. Share your ambivalence with each other. Express both sides. "I'm grateful that you pick up the ball with the children's activities while I'm still at work. Yet I find myself holding on to some of the responsibilities that you are willing to do. I'm conflicted about my role as a good mother."

Or how about this one: "Honey, I find your suggestion that I check the Sunday paper and the Internet for job possibilities a great annoyance, and yet I also know that it's coming from a loving, caring place in your heart."

When we reveal our feelings to each other, we feel connected on a more intimate level.

I will tell you my needs and desires.

Another level of revealing ourselves involves expressing our needs in and desires for our relationship. Just because your mate expresses a desire doesn't mean that you have to meet that desire. It does mean that you need to consider the request. Behind that request there is important information about your spouse that you need to discover. At that point you may choose to completely meet the request, to partially meet it, or not to meet it at all.

We assume you will communicate clearly if you are unable to meet it. Perhaps that would be a good time to raise an alternative possibility. "Honey, my schedule doesn't allow me to pick up the clothes from the cleaners today. I will be happy to do it first thing tomorrow morning. Would that work for you?"

I will tell you what I need and like sexually.

We have very specific needs and desires in the sexual area. They are often challenging to talk about. A deeper level of intimacy happens when we reveal those needs and desires.

A Redbook magazine survey of more than 100,000 married women, the largest of its kind, determined that the strongest indicator of sexual and marital satisfaction among women was "the ability to express sexual feelings to their husband. The more they talked about their sexual relationship, the better they rated their sex lives, their marriages, and their overall happiness."[3]

Contrary to popular belief, talking about sex doesn't "destroy the magic." It makes the magic come alive. When we don't talk, monogamy often turns into monotony. We please each other best by being honest about what is pleasurable to us.

Expecting your husband or wife to know what you want is like going to a restaurant and expecting the waiter to guess what you are going to order. Speaking up builds trust, shows you care, shows you are invested in your relationship, increases your personal honesty, and begins the transformation of your sexual relationship.

Many couples don't ever talk about sex. Others try to talk, but they talk around sex, not directly about it. We need to assume responsibility for communicating our sexual needs and feelings so that we alleviate any guessing games.

Paul writes in 1 Corinthians 7:3-5 (*The Message*): "The marriage bed must be a place of mutuality—the husband seeking to satisfy his wife, the wife seeking to satisfy her husband. Marriage is not a place to stand up for your rights. Marriage is a decision to serve the other, whether in bed or out." The marriage bed can never be a place of mutuality if you don't understand and talk about the differing needs you have sexually.

Differing Sexual Needs

Wife	Husband
Stimulated by touch and tender words	Stimulated visually
Needs love to open up to sex	Needs sex to open up to love
Needs to relax and get into sex slowly	Starts out all ready to go
Needs great communication to enjoy sex	Sex opens a man up to his feelings; sex precedes communication
Needs time to enjoy sex	Needs an occasional "quickie."
Pleasure is increased by direct stimulation of nonerogenous zones first	Pleasure is increased by direct stimulation of erogenous zones first
Pleasure corresponds to a gradual build-up of tension	Experiences pleasure as a release of sexual tension.
Orgasm results from direct stimulation of the clitoris, not only through sexual intercourse	Orgasms from direct or oral stimulation of penis and testicles
Doesn't always need orgasm to feel fulfilled	Needs orgasm to feel fulfilled
Enjoyment increases when she focuses on the sensations in her body	Enjoyment increases when he focuses on his wife enjoying sex
After orgasm, still aroused	After orgasm, loses arousal quickly

A good sexual relationship is actually a work in progress. Men, you need to strive to understand your wives' wants and desires. For many women a major component of sex is the level of non-sexual intimacy in the relationship.

Women, you need to understand that many men are

performance oriented and that the sexual act itself is important to them.

Each partner must be ready to enter the other's world. We must tell each other what we need and like sexually. We must learn how to respond to each other's needs.

I will let you know the impact your choices have on me.

We impact each other in a myriad of meaningful ways. A kind word, a warm, loving time of physical intimacy, an unexpected kindness all add up to a smile in your spouse's heart.

The challenge comes when you have to cope with the negative impact of the words your mate has said, or actions he or she has done. If you don't speak up, your negative feelings begin to fester. Jesus makes it clear that no matter who caused the problem, you need to take steps to solve it (Matthew 5:23–24; 18:15).

We need to give the problem a forum in which it can be resolved. When we don't, anxiety, discontent, and the potential to magnify disrupt our love story.

When Jeff and Laurie got married, they made a verbal commitment to use a phrase of connection whenever there was a difficult issue to talk about. They would say, "Because I love you and care about our relationship, there are some difficult things I need to share. . . ." They discovered over the years that the key was to use "word patrol." They made sure that they stayed in the "I" mode.

Contrast this honest expression of anger: "*When you don't let me know you're going to be late, I get very concerned about where you are and whether you're all right. I feel afraid. Then when you do get home, I'm relieved that you're safe, but still upset that you seem to care so little for my feelings*" to this tirade: "*I don't see how, if you loved me, you could just let me sit here for hours worrying about whether you're in some ditch, bleeding to death. You are totally self-centered and inconsiderate. You never think of my feelings at all.*"

The Apostle Paul admonishes us, "Do not let any unwholesome

talk come out of your mouths, but only what is helpful for building others up according to their needs, that it may benefit those who listen" (Ephesians 4:29).

Direct or Indirect Communication

It is crucial that we speak from an "I" position. If we do that we will get to the heart of the matter, and we won't indirectly use jokes, offhand comments, or sarcasm.

Jim and Joan had a problem. They used to spend Monday nights as a date night, that is, before Jim joined a men's Bible study on Monday evening. Joan could use indirect communication. She could talk to him but not really address the issue. For example, "Jim, how can you leave? There are so many chores that need to be done around here."

Another indirect approach might be to ask, "Is it totally necessary for you to spend every Monday with your friends?" Or, she might try a guilt trip: "You are neglecting our family, Jim." We sincerely doubt that any of these indirect attempts would have a productive ending.

Instead she could be direct in her communication and say, "I miss our date nights on Mondays. I know you are enjoying this men's study, yet I find myself resenting it. I'd like us to consider setting aside another evening for a regular date time. Would you be interested?"

Obviously, her husband would respond best to the positive, direct request.

I will clarify my limits.

Another important way that we reveal ourselves involves clarifying and setting limits with each other.

"Honey, would you like to make love tonight?"

How would your marriage handle that question? Is it okay to say "no" in your relationship? If you aren't free in your marriage to

> Kind words can be short and easy to speak, but their echoes are truly endless.

express your "no," then your "yes" is meaningless.

On the other hand, if you are constantly saying no to your mate's sexual advances, then there are severe problems in your relationship. We recommend that you see a Christian professional, a pastor, or a counselor if this has become your pattern.

The way we say "no" is important. If our no is abrupt, it feels like rejection. We suggest that a no be accompanied by an alternative, like this.

"Honey, would you like to make love tonight?"

"A part of me would love to make love, but I have a deadline I have to meet for work, so I would like to suggest that we reserve Friday night for a romantic unhurried time together."

When the no is followed by an alternative, it is still disappointing, but it demonstrates to your mate that he or she is desired and that you are invested in your sexual relationship. On this occasion, the invitation did not come at a suitable time.

Don't let your spouse be a travel agent for guilt trips. If in the past you always collapsed and gave in, don't assume that you have to give an immediate answer. Take a time-out of one hour to think about this. Give yourself some privacy to think. Then give your answer. These are your choices:

Say "no" to the request and suggest an alternative time.

Say "no" to the request and suggest another solution.

Say "no" graciously, firmly, and without guilt if the suggestion is totally unacceptable to you.

If one of you is more sexually conservative, that person should decide the guidelines for your sexual relationship. It's a violation to push your partner into any act that he or she is uncomfortable with. We could even call it "marital rape." Mind you, we do hope that the more conservative partner will be open to taking small steps out of his or her comfort zone to experience the freedom that

God desires for us within our marriage relationship.

Anything out of control harms your marriage. There are times that you have to be willing to be unpopular and say "no." Limits need to be set by loving spouses on uncontrolled anger (Proverbs 29:11), uncontrolled lust (Proverbs 6:32), uncontrolled spending (Proverbs 21:20), uncontrolled drinking (Proverbs 23:29,30; Proverbs 20:1), uncontrolled ambition (Proverbs 23:4), uncontrolled laziness (Proverbs 28:19), and uncontrolled denial around parenting issues (Proverbs 3:11,12).

When you clarify your limits, you tell your partner what is acceptable and what isn't. People often behave as poorly as others will tolerate. We must take responsibility for communicating what is not acceptable to us. (For more on this subject, we highly recommend the book *Boundaries in Marriage* by John Townsend and Henry Cloud.[4])

I will confess my faults and mistakes.

The last way we reveal ourselves to each other is by getting honest about our mistakes and faults.

When you lay an egg, hold it up. Own it as your own.

Never spoil an apology with an excuse. "Love from the center of who you are; don't fake it" (Romans 12:9, *The Message*). Being accountable for one's own shortcomings requires personal humility. When we confess our faults to each other, when we share a part of ourselves that we fear, are confused about, hate, or are ashamed of, we take our intimacy to a new depth.

We naturally assume that if we let our mates see our weaknesses, they won't like us. This logic is as old as Adam and Eve. When they broke away from love and disobeyed God, they hid. No longer were they comfortable revealing who they were to each other.

Many times we feel afraid to share our failure for fear of losing our partner's respect.

Nancy heard the announcement in church. A new support

group was forming for women who had previously had an abortion. She really wanted to attend. She knew she still struggled with incredible guilt. She had never told anyone her dark secret. At times when her husband would hug her and tell her that he adored her, she would cringe inside and think, If he only knew. Her husband, Jack, was very active in the pro-life movement. He often shared his grief over the choices young women were making. Could she risk telling him? Would he lose all respect for her?

Finally Nancy got up her courage and told Jack about her abortion. It had happened years ago before she became a Christian. She had just come over from England and was completely alone in a foreign country. As she talked to her husband, all the pain of twenty years started to flow. Tears streamed down her cheeks. All Jack could do was hold her in his arms and weep with her. When he assured her of his love and support, her sobs became gut wrenching. He had no idea that she had carried such pain and guilt all these years. As partners, Jack and Nancy took her shame and guilt to Jesus. In Christ's presence they began together "to feel and understand . . . how long, how wide, how deep and how high [God's} love really is; and to experience this love for [themselves] . . . so at last [they were] filled up with God Himself" (Ephesians 3:18-19, TLB).

Nancy felt closer to Jack than she had ever felt. He knew her deepest shame and still loved her. Nancy's vulnerability freed him up to share his greatest shame with her. He had gotten a young woman pregnant his freshman year of college. Together they had decided to give the baby up for adoption. He felt such agony about his failure. He had been a Christian at the time this had happened. Nancy opened her arms to him. That day they both experienced a new level of intimacy.

It is our imperfections and our pain that draw us close to each other. It is hard to entrust someone with your faults and mistakes unless you see in that person a matching willingness to be vulnerable and you are confident you won't be judged.

Honesty about who we are makes our connection real. It makes our need for God real and it makes us real.

Decision #10
"I Will Reveal Myself to You"

For Reflection and Discussion

1. The following questions are designed to help you begin revealing yourself to your spouse. Why don't you take one or two questions on your date nights over the next several months?

Who were your role models growing up?

How did they handle emotions?

What did you learn from them about speaking your truth?

Did your parents speak their truth?

What consequences did you experience for honesty?

Growing up were there certain feelings that were taboo?

What were they?

Do you have difficulty expressing or hearing those feelings now? Explain.

How would you describe your parents' relationship with each other?

What did you learn about relationship from your parents?

What did you learn that you desire to keep in your marriage?

What do you want to avoid?

How did your dating relationships shape you?

2. If you have been married before, what did you learn about revealing yourself and your feelings in that relationship?

3. Is it difficult for you to be upset and still stay emotionally connected with your spouse? Why?

4. Do you find yourself reacting to your mate as you reacted to a significant person in your childhood? Explain.

What is your fondest relational memory growing up?

What is a deep hurt that you carry from your childhood . . . your adolescence . . . or your early twenties?

How did your past shape you into the person you are today? Explain.

5. Rank your top ten desires.

__ I want to know that you are in our marriage for life.
__ I want to be able to trust your words and actions.
__ I want you to respect my ideas even if you don't agree.
__ I want you to say no when that is your truth.
__ I want to know that disagreement and differing perspectives are welcome in our marriage.
__ I want you to speak your truth even if I might end up with hurt feelings.
__ I want to be affectionately touched on a regular basis without it leading to sex.
__ I want to have regular times of sexual intimacy.
__ I want to know specific ways that I am important to you.
__ I want to be included in our financial decisions.
__ I want to know that I am a partner in decision-making.
__ I would like you to express words of connection and love at the same time that you are raising issues of concern.
__ I want to be able to express my feelings and fears.
__ I want to have regular high quality time alone with you.
__ I want more personal space in our marriage.
__ I want to hear you express your love to me regularly.
__ I want to feel valued and important to you.
__ I want to be able to trust that you will discuss our problems with me rather than talking behind my back with others.
__ I want to know that together we are growing spiritually.
__ I want to be able to take a time-out in the midst of conflict in order to gain personal control. I will return to talk in one hour.
__ I want to introduce you to the significant support people in my life.
__ I want to hear you say, "I was wrong" or "Please forgive me, I'm sorry I caused you pain."

After selecting your top ten desires, sit down together and

share each desire one at a time and what it would specifically look like in your marriage. For example, "I would feel more important to you if you would phone me from work when you are going to arrive home later than you had previously planned."

If one of your top ten needs is already being fulfilled in your marriage, celebrate it. Let each other know how it is being met.

6. Discuss with each other what facts on the sexual needs chart in this chapter apply to you. How would you like your spouse to support you? Be specific.

7. Are you direct or indirect when you raise a difficult issue? Do your words build or undermine your relationship? Focus on an example from this last month.

8. Would you and your partner like to make any changes in the way you address difficult issues? If so, how?

DECISION ELEVEN

"I Will Allow You to Influence Me"

In the last few months, has your spouse communicated something to you that you are choosing to ignore? This letter was anonymously faxed to our office.

Dear Dave and Jan:

My problem is that my husband has always complained that he is the aggressor when it comes to sex, and he is generally right. We both work and have a very busy schedule. We also have two beautiful children who require lots of attention. We manage to work things out quite well when it comes to juggling schedules, taking the kids to soccer practice and karate, trying to come together for dinner, and just being a normal family. It's hectic most of the time and pretty hard, but we manage. By the time we get to bed, I am exhausted.

My husband is ready for sex as soon as I get to bed, but I just want to relax and unwind. I have expressed that the mood would help me out, like candles, music, a nice massage, but none of this ever happens unless I set it up. So we basically have sex, and he is happy and I am left unsatisfied and feeling used. It's hard to talk to him about this because when I have tried, he says I'm the one with the problem.

One night recently, I decided to abandon the sweatpants and comfortable shirt I normally sleep in, surprise my husband, and put on a sexy nightgown. He was relaxing in the den, and the kids were with relatives for the weekend. I got all dolled up, put on perfume, and walked into the den feeling like one of those angels on the Victoria Secret commercial. My husband just looked at me, then turned his head and continued to watch television. He did not comment on how I looked or anything. I waited for a while, but my husband was into his TV show. I read a magazine. Later, he dozed off to sleep, so I got up and went and put my pajamas on. I have learned over the years that he doesn't compliment me much. I have gotten compliments from outsiders, and they are reassuring, but it would be great to hear a few from my husband.

A Hurting Wife

Can you feel the agony in this letter? This husband may have heard his wife's request, but he was in no way willing to be influenced by her words.

Early in most relationships we hang on every word that our lovers speak. Then at some point we lose our commitment to listen, our commitment to hear each other.

Intimacy Blockers

Sometimes the more we need love the more we block love. We make it extremely difficult for our mates to approach us. The higher the walls we build, the less our chances of letting love touch or transform us.

"A man's mind stretched by a new idea can never go back to its original dimensions."

We block influence in a multitude of ways. One is to assume that there is nothing more to know. Another is to decide that change is impossible. When we give up we stop listening. At that point, we are blinded by our labels.

It seemed to Ruth that every time she talked to Darren about money, he would get upset. After months of futile attempts to discuss their financial situation, Ruth started to see her husband as an angry person. If fact, she even labeled him as abusive and began to wonder how she could have married someone with such a severe character flaw.

What Ruth neglected to notice was that Darren was able to talk to others about money without getting angry. She never asked herself, "Why does he find it difficult to talk to me about money? What is my part in this?" Instead, she overlooked the exception because of her condemning spirit.

Whatever we focus on gains a strong influence in our life. When we label our mates as angry, unaffectionate, or oversexed, we fail to notice any behavior that deviates from our perception. We have blinders on. As Norman Cousins said, "We fear the worst, we expect the worst, and we invite the worst."[1] All of our energy is expended trying to make the other person wrong. When we do this we deny that we have any role in the creation of a painful relationship. In Jesus' words, "Why do you look at the speck of sawdust in your brother's eye and pay no attention to the plank in your own eye?" (Matthew 7:3).

When a relationship is in trouble, people tend to analyze. The analysis, however, usually turns "the other guy" into the problem. Our microscope is too narrowly focused, leading to a cesspool of mutual recrimination, blame ("be lame"), and misunderstanding.

There are many other actions we take that effectively block intimacy.

Pre-judging

"What is prejudice? An opinion, which is not based upon reason; a judgment, without having heard the argument; a feeling, without being able to trace whence it came" (Carrie Chapman Catt).[2]

The attractive middle-aged couple sat on the counseling couch. Ryan informed us that his wife hadn't voted in the presidential election. Then he went into an eloquent monologue about how this proved her intellectual inferiority. She just wasn't interest in having a worldview. By contrast, he was fascinated by politics, history, and philosophy.

Bianca had heard more than she wanted to hear. With her eyes flashing, she looked at us and said that if we believed Ryan's analysis, we would have a completely faulty perception.

Prior to hearing Bianca's explanation, we suggested that Ryan would find a greater degree of success if he would ask her questions with the intent of understanding rather than attempting to confirm his preconceived opinion.

Together we discovered that Bianca had been in business meetings from early morning until 6 p.m. She ran a multi-million - dollar business. When she exited the meeting with the intention of voting, one of her managers approached her. The woman was extremely upset and teary. Bianca spent the next hour with her. When the manager left, Bianca asked an employee when the polls closed. She was told seven o'clock, so she went home. Only later did she discover that the polls actually closed at 8 p.m.

The more Ryan judged, the less he loved and the less he understood his wife's world.

A husband whose wife was constantly misinterpreting his intentions gave her a small frame with these words mounted in it.

I will never intentionally hurt you.

I do not have to be right.

I can be influenced.

I have no desire to rule over you or control you.

It is safe to admit you are wrong to me.

I will never use it against you.

I will not be unfaithful to you.

I love you and will continue loving you.

As his wife read these statements over the next few months, she started to question her judgments instead of her husband's intentions.

Preaching

Sometimes one spouse uses Scripture to force a point. "Let me share this verse with you . . . " is another way of saying, "I can't tolerate your feelings, and I'm about to lay the whole matter to rest by nailing you."

Or how about "The Lord must be trying to tell you something"? This amounts to a guilt trip—or worse, a bad case of a spouse trying to read God's mind.

A husband who had been regularly thumping his wife on the head with the Bible told us, "I was always trying to give back the right answer—to correct her—instead of being her friend." His wife had her bags packed and was leaving. She not only rejected him, she rejected the God of his making.

Taking over the other person's story

When you share your heart, and your listener interrupts you to say that a similar thing happened to him or her, your story is no longer yours. The focus shifts to the listener who interrupted you. You are left out in the cold.

Disqualifing the other person's feelings

Tyrone wanted to pull his hair out. Whenever he would risk venturing into the unfamiliar world of feelings, his well-meaning wife would step in with her analysis. Either she'd tell him that he wasn't feeling "angry," he must be feeling "hurt," or she'd tell him, "You shouldn't feel that way." She would set herself up as the judge of what his internal world was. Hidden in her reaction was the assumption that feelings must always be logical, rational, and controlled.

Minimizing the other person's pain

More and more we seem to have become numb to the suffering of others and ashamed of our own suffering. Yet suffering is one of the universal conditions of being alive.

When Christie would bring her pain to her husband, he'd tell her, "It isn't that bad, honey. Think positively. It will turn out okay. Things could be worse. God doesn't give us more than we can handle."

Then Christie felt guilty for feeling discouraged and down. To her this was a serious issue. She felt minimized and alone. It seemed to her that her husband didn't want to be bothered with anything that wasn't happy. He seemed callous to her concerns. She also knew that sometimes things don't work out. Failure and tragedy are real. His platitudes led her to feel as if she didn't have a companion on life's journey.

Interrupting

Sometimes we're guilty of grasshopper listening. We listen only long enough to hear what we expect. Then we jump in with our two cents, or we race off thinking we have understood. This leaves one's partner feeling frustrated, isolated, and invisible.

"He who answers before listening," says the writer of Proverbs, "that is his folly and his shame" (Proverbs 18:13).

Coming up with quick solutions

Fast advice usually addresses a false problem. People want us to listen. When we do and we validate their feelings, they believe we are trustworthy. When we quickly offer solutions, they are often left irritated.

Cheryl was upset. She enjoyed her role as PTA president at her daughter's school. There were times she just needed to vent. People could be challenging. Deadlines weren't always honored. Whenever she would attempt to share her frustrations with Mark, he'd give the same reply: "Quit." She was put out.

When I ask you to listen to me and you start giving advice,
You have not done what I asked.
When I ask you to listen to me and you feel you have to
do something to solve my problems, you have failed me,

strange as that may seem . . .
So please, just listen and hear me.
And if you want to talk, Wait a few moments for your turn
and I promise I'll listen to you.
- Anonymous

Living defensively

It is possible to live so defensively that we never love at all. Instead of loving, we relate to one another by using defense mechanisms. Defensive interchanges are somewhat like a Teflon pan—we're so slippery that no one can connect with us. There is no possibility of another's influence sticking. A very popular mechanism is the counterattack.

Sometimes one partner becomes like a district attorney proving guilt to a jury, going for the mate's jugular. If attacks and counterattacks have become your pattern, perhaps these words ring true. As one husband said, "I began to realize that by the end of a day of work, I'd get an upset stomach knowing that in a couple of hours I'd have to go home."

Anger can give an illusion of power. If we rage, we don't have to feel helpless, hurt, or needy. Instead of asking for comfort because we're afraid, we become gruff and sarcastic, and we push each other away. The trouble is that a sharp tongue cuts any possibility of connection.

Jeremy described his reality with these words. "When I feel out of control I become nervous and angry. It gets much worse if I am under stress. When triggered, I can go into a full-blown white-hot rage within a fraction of a second. I want to hurt my wife because she's hurt me."

When your spouse states a perspective, you might accuse him or her of being a liar because the viewpoint is different from yours. At that point you slam the door on any possibility of influence.

"Nothing lowers the level of conversation more than raising your voice."

Becoming competitive

John came dragging through the door at seven o'clock at night. He greeted Dianne with these words: "I've had the most horrendous day. It was a hard one." Instead of learning about her husband's day, however, Dianne shot back, "I've had a hard day, too. You're not the only one who works around here. In fact, when you get home so late you make my load greater."

Couples end up competing about amazing things. Who is the most exhausted, the most intelligent, the most sexual, the most communicative, the most "sick." The list can go on and on and on. When we compete, we block connection.

Making differences "wrong"

Men may be from Mars and women from Venus according to author John Gray, but both sexes reside on planet Earth, and we need to learn how to embrace each other's uniqueness if we are ever going to be influenced by one another.

> "A hot-tempered person stirs up dissension; a patient person calms a quarrel."

The Smiths decided to rent a video one Friday evening. They made a big batch of popcorn, started the fire in their fireplace, and snuggled in for a time of relaxation. As they watched the video, Jim was feeling connected and close. On the other hand, June was miserable. In order to feel connection, June wanted to talk. She started to accuse her husband of not caring about their relationship, of being passive and unapproachable. Jim didn't know what happened. He just knew the evening was ruined because she was so critical and demanding. Neither understood what the other needed, and so they made each other mad.

Shutting each other down

The new word of choice for blocking influence seems to be "Whatever." Then we walk out on each other either emotionally or physically.

Women are often the emotional regulators of the marriage, although there are always exceptions to that rule. When they feel distance, they often start to pursue their husbands. At times they may use criticism to connect. It's been said that "a man may be a fool and not know it, but not if he's married."

Men have radar against control, so they often withdraw and ignore their wives' attempts. The reality is that a man really needs to worry when his wife doesn't pursue anymore. She will be moving toward indifference . . . and indifference is the opposite of love.

In his excellent book, *Getting the Love You Want*, Harville Hendrix created a long list of ways that each of us "exits" our relationship. Every time we use one of these exits, we block the possibility of our partners' influence.[3]

Reading romance novels
Staying late at work
Spending too much time with the children
Overeating
Disappearing into the garage
Camping on the phone
Continually washing and waxing the car
Volunteering for every committee at church, school, etc.
Spending too much time with a hobby
Spending time at Mom's
Having an affair
Avoiding eye contact
Memorizing every word of the newspaper
Falling asleep on the couch
Being a sports junkie
Coming home late for dinner

Fantasizing while making love
Being sick and tired all the time
Not wanting to be touched
Overindulgence in alcoholic drinks and drugs
Lying
Refusing to make love
Having sex but not making love
Living on the tennis court or golf course
Bulimia
Jogging ten miles a day
Going on weekend fishing trips
Going shopping
Daydreaming
Refusing to talk
Working on the house all the time
Masturbating
Playing guitar
Keeping separate bank accounts
Picking fights
Spending hours on the computer
Reading magazines
Doing crossword puzzles
Watching movies

Blocked Intimacy

An articulate woman expressed her feelings to her husband, who had very effectively blocked her influence for fifteen years: "I was left angry. I felt controlled, as if I didn't have choice, and yet I knew I was an adult. I felt trapped. It resulted in my feeling combative. I had to fight for my right to exist. I needed to be acknowledged. By denying me freedom of expression, you made me want freedom more.

"I became a shell of a person. I felt empty, hurt, isolated, and alone. When I tried to talk to you, it was as if I was talking into a tunnel. How disconnected I felt from you. It used to be you and me against the world. No more—now it was all about you.

"I felt screwed up. Feelings are just feelings, yet you judged mine and criticized me for them and labeled me because of them. I felt tired and crushed. After one of our arguments, I feel frantic. Is my only choice to drown? I can't breathe. I'm threatened. I'm losing myself. I don't want you to define the feelings that are acceptable, the decisions that you approve of. I feel cheated and gypped. I've lost out. I want to escape. Most of all, I feel lost and overwhelmed."

Now we want to share portions of a letter written by Thomas Jones, a pastor, thirteen years after his divorce. From the perspective of hindsight, he created a letter of warning to husbands.

> I was preoccupied. As we got down to the hard business of married life, it was a fact that for all my idealism about marriage, I was too busy to be a good husband. There was simply no time for my wife. Even when we were together, my mind was generally somewhere else. I wasn't listening.
>
> But what I failed to see then—and for a long time afterward—was that I was doing all the talking. I was sharing my wonderful world with her, but there was not any room in me for what was happening in her world. Actually, and this is hard for me to admit even now, her world was not very interesting to me.
>
> Through it all I failed to ever grasp what my wife had understood early in our marriage. I failed to see that my life, my priorities, my career, my personal growth had become the only things that mattered enough to cause me to take significant action.[4]

One of the tasks of marriage is that we have to learn how to tolerate and welcome our partners' influence. Some fake orgasm, others go through their married life faking feelings and connection.

When Jesus was here on earth, He made it His priority to build His life into twelve men, the disciples. All but one of the disciples were dramatically changed by being around Christ. Judas wouldn't open himself up to Christ's influence.

When we block all influence, we have a serious character flaw. Arrogance rules our life, humility does not. Instead of holding our perspective as a hypothesis, we cling to it as the absolute truth. Solomon spoke wisely when he told us that "pride only breeds quarrels." The *Good News Bible* translates it this way: "Arrogance causes nothing but trouble" (Proverbs 13:10).

What might an attitude of humility look like? Perhaps you'd remind yourself that your conclusion is not necessarily absolute truth. You'd acknowledge that your mate is a separate person. You don't know everything about him. You don't know her every thought and feeling. You'd question the impact you are having on your spouse. You'd say yes to differences. You'd remind yourself that you are imperfect, fully capable of being wrong.

Yes, you are capable of sin. You might even ask yourself how you contributed to the problem you are both dealing with at this time. In fact, you might be more concerned that your partner's needs are being met in your marriage than your own. You'd put more effort into making sure that his or her interests are heard, valued, and addressed. You will have comprehended at a deep level Paul's admonition, "Do nothing out of selfish ambition or vain conceit, but in humility consider others better than yourselves. Each of you should look not only to your own interests, but also to the interests of others" (Philippians 2:3,4).

Building Intimacy

We suspect that the most basic, powerful, and loving way to connect with one's spouse is to listen. Perhaps the most important thing we give one another other is our attention. How we listen is the strongest way that we show our partners that we are willing to be influenced. A great listener has the rare ability to make others feel as if each of them is the only person in the world.

Listening is an art. One woman put it this way: "Listening is the oldest and most powerful tool of healing. It is often through the quality of our listening and not the wisdom of our words that we are able to effect the most profound changes in the people around us. Our listening creates sanctuary for the homeless parts within the other person. That which has been denied, unloved, and devalued by themselves and others. Listening creates a holy silence. When you listen generously to people, they can hear truth in themselves often for the first time. And in the silence of listening you can know yourself in everyone."[5]

There is no more wonderful gift than attention given from the heart. When we seek to understand others, we receive them, we take them in, and we demonstrate that we care deeply about them. Concentrating completely on your spouse is the best way to make him or her feel significant.

Often we get difficult and hostile when we feel that we aren't being heard. Many disagreements would stop if one mate would simply acknowledge the other's feelings and point of view. Listening is an investment in your partner's life. It says, "You are not alone. I am here with you." Make it your life mission to really understand each other's feelings, desires, and needs. You must remain as stubbornly interested in hearing your partner's perspective as you are in voicing your own. If you're not listening, you're not learning.

Real-life Stories of Influence

It seems to be a fact of life and relationship that in order to have influence with others we have to be willing to be influenced by them. Amazing miracles happen when we open ourselves up to each other's influence. In many ways we tangibly feel God's loving touch on our lives.

Philip Yancey shares how his wife taught him the meaning of love. "I wonder if I could ever have learned to love God had I not learned first, through her, to love. If we become persons through relationship, the person I am today is due in large measure to her. Painfully shy, socially inept, emotionally damaged though I was when I met her, she nevertheless looked past those handicaps and graced me with her love and attention. She is visiting her family two thousand miles away as I write these words, and yet she 'lives' inside me. All day long I have felt her absence as a kind of presence."[6]

Husband and author Joel Achenbach wrote an article for *Redbook* magazine entitled "What Men Secretly Love About Marriage." He shares how as a bachelor he used paper towels instead of napkins. They worked; they were just folded differently. In fact, he questioned why anyone would consider buying napkins when he could get a giant roll of paper towels at a much better price. Things have changed in the Achenbach home since Mary entered. They now use "Mary-sanctioned napkins," and Joel has to admit that they feel a lot nicer on his face than a paper towel did.

We laughed as we read the article. Influence can be a wonderful thing.

Joel continues, "One of the worst things about being single is the continuation of the cult of the self. I'm happy to say that I am no longer wrapped up with the obsession with this one particular person who happened to be me. I now have Mary and our three daughters—people for whom I'd sacrifice my life. I am thrilled to know my wife."[7]

Dr. David Seamands, a pastor, teacher, author, and missionary, shares about the freedom and transformation that came to their marriage when finally he opened himself up to his wife's influence. "We were in India, and through a converging of nationalism, Hinduism, and communism we had to leave a certain area just as I was drowning in my own successes. We were at the heart of a mass movement; I was baptizing three thousand new believers a year—a rare privilege for a young man in his twenties. We were building a new church every month. I had said, 'This is my dream; we're going to stay here for a lifetime.' It was a miniature Pentecost.

"But God knew better. I would have been the biggest phony in the world if we had stayed there. When we were forced out, I really hit bottom. Until then, my wife had always seemed a bit on the weepy side, and so I had thought, *My goodness, if I tell her what's bugging me about the church or the mission station—that it's getting to the lonely scared boy inside of me—we'll go down the tube together.* I didn't dare tell her. I felt I had to play the strong role.

"Actually, she wasn't weak; she was just expressive. The moment that I revealed my weakness, the most amazing thing happened. She said, 'My goodness, I never knew whether you needed me.' Suddenly, she opened up like a flower to the sun and became the strong person she had always been. I only had to let her know she was needed. I allowed her to minister to me."[8]

A precious couple we were working with faced a major challenge. The wife was struggling with recurring intrusive memories as a result of being sexually abused by her father as a very young child. Their sex life was suffering because she would shut down during their lovemaking times. We suggested that they would benefit from "eyes open" intimacy. Anytime she had a flashback, she was to turn on the lights, and then they were to hold each other and look into each other's eyes until the anxiety quieted. She was to touch her husband's face and say his name and acknowledge that she was choosing to be intimate with him. Over time, as this couple learned to inhale each other's love deep into their being, their lovemaking became a beautiful and treasured part of their marriage.

John Wooden, the former UCLA basketball coach who won ten NCAA championships turned ninety on October 15, 2000. Bill Plasche wrote an article in the *Los Angeles Times* honoring the coach. We were profoundly touched as we read about the effect his wife, Nell, had had on John when she was alive.

Mr. Wooden lives in a condominium, in a place darkened by piles of books and trophies and photos, because Nell is there. "My children have wanted me to come live with them, but everything here reminds me of Nell," he said of his wife of fifty-three years, who died in 1985. "Everything on the wall, she put there. The bookcases were her idea. The white carpet, she picked out . . . ."

He said that he still writes letters to Nell on the twenty-first of each month, the day she died. The love notes have been carefully bundled together and rest on the pillow next to his.

"I haven't been afraid of death since I lost Nell," Mr. Wooden says. "I tell myself, this is the only chance I'll have to be with her again."[9]

Perhaps you've experienced the synergy of working together toward a common goal. Together you have challenged each other to move forward rather than holding each other back. Has your spouse taught you to appreciate interests you never had before the relationship—like classical music, hockey games, plants, travel, natural beauty, and physical exercise? Have you seen the world differently as a result of looking through each other's eyes? Perhaps you now look at the world through compassionate eyes as a result of welcoming your spouse's influence.

We asked precious friends to tell us one way that they had been influenced by each other over the thirty years of their marriage.

Husband: "My wife has kept me active doing things, seeking adventure beyond what my energy level would be on my own. She is a young woman at fifty."

Wife: "My husband grew up in a home where everyone was welcome—the more the merrier. Fabulous food, music, a revolving door of dinner guests and houseguests was his norm. During the early years of marriage I was reluctant to entertain, inviting no more than four guests at a time. Over the years, with my husband's influence and encouragement, our home has become a gathering ground for our kids, their friends, our friends and family. I am inspired and sustained, in part, by entertaining. The more the merrier."

The Test of Influence

We believe that God has much to teach us through each other. You cannot truly know yourself until you observe how you relate to your spouse. A relationship is like a mirror. As you interact with your partner, you learn about yourself. At that point, "Intimacy becomes more than satisfaction, it becomes a revelation."[10]

Solomon, if we can put a couple of words into his mouth, put it this way, "As iron sharpens iron, so one [spouse] sharpens another" (Proverbs 27:17).

The hardest time to allow influence is when your partner needs to express frustration, anger, and/or criticism. Perhaps one of us has sinned against the other (losing one's temper, losing self-control, having a judgmental attitude, exhibiting out-of-control behavior, being dishonest, abusing power, and showing pride, just to mention a few possibilities). Perhaps one of us has hurt feelings and needs to share. What is your track record for receiving this input?

Do you value even unhappy input coming from your mate, or do you immediately go on the defensive? Are you open to feedback and correction? Many of us fight the truth and each other, rather than fighting the problem.

"He who ignores discipline despises himself, but whoever heeds correction gains understanding" (Proverbs 15:32).

"No discipline seems pleasant at the time but painful. Later on, however, it produces a harvest of righteousness and peace for those who have been trained by it" (Hebrews 12:11).

Attitude of Influence

When your spouse has hurt your feelings or sinned against you, it is natural to believe that he or she is your problem. As we have mentioned, that is an arrogant and dishonest stance to take. Partners are equal in value in our loving Father's eyes. Both are imperfect and immature human beings in need of a Savior. We have been leveled at the cross. If one suffers, so does the other.

> "Our mutual surrenders have caused us to grow rather than to shrink."

Accept your partner with an open heart. Deal with the issue.

Our choices are not dependent on being treated well first. As we understand Scripture, not one of us can rationalize returning evil for evil. We are to be kind and compassionate to one another. We are to be "holy" in reaction. That may involve allowing our partners to go into rehabilitation, or even to jail, but always out of a loving commitment to their growth, not out of revenge and one-upmanship.

Men and Women of Influence

The astronaut John Glenn encouraged his wife's interest in a course at Hollins College in Roanoke, Virginia, for people who stuttered. The class was successful. One day when he got home she said, "John, I've wanted to tell you this for years: pick up your socks." They laughed, embraced each other, and he picked up his socks.[10]

A woman's desire to talk about their relationship may threaten her husband. He may not be as adept at sharing his inner experience as she is. She wants more even if she translates "more" into a one-sentence positive request—such as "I would like you to give me your undivided attention when I tell you something that is on my heart"—he may feel criticized. He may retreat into his "cave" and feel justified because a popular speaker says that normal men do that.

She feels crazy and caught in a double bind. If she asks for what she needs and he gets defensive, there is a detached distance between them. If she doesn't ask, nothing will change. Often she's also afraid if she gives her husband space, he'll never come her way for connection. The result is that both of them feel misunderstood and distant.

Men today long for an emotional life, not because their wives are pushing them, but for themselves. Clients tell of tears coming to their eyes when they hear stories of men who have had the courage to get off the treadmill of corporate life to follow their dreams, their passion. Many men have a sense that they have missed out on life while they've been caught up in making a living. They also feel caught in a dilemma. They long to share their feelings, but if they do, will their wives see them as weak?

Jan: Women, we need to release our frustration, anger, resentment, and feelings of being superior in communication. We need to approach our husbands with empathy and understanding. Questioning is really a listening rather than a speaking skill; one that we, as women, need to develop. We need to question with the intent of understanding rather than arguing.

Phrases both husbands and wives could benefit from using are:

Tell me more . . .

I want to understand why you feel this way.

How important is this to you?

If that had happened to me, I might have felt . . .

Do you have any of those feelings?

Any time we hear emotion, we need to use the above questions. We listen to understand. We receive the deep, sacred communication of a separate, unique human being.

Listen for feelings as well as content. Then check your understanding. In your own words, let your mate know what you've heard on the feeling and the content level. In this way, you check out your understanding and give your partner a chance to respond, "No, that's not quite what I was trying to say. This is what I meant." This process lets your spouse know that he or she has been heard.

For many men, this process of giving feedback will feel like speaking a foreign language. It may seem awkward. Women can facilitate their husbands' attempts by graciously receiving their words.

It is normal for men to need separateness, time to withdraw, space-out, or to become consumed by an activity or project. Women must guard against personalizing this. Accept your husband; don't attempt to reform him. Listening is a profound way that we can embrace Paul's admonition in Ephesians 5:33: "However, let each man of you [without exception] love his wife as [being in a sense] his very own self; and let the wife see that she respects and reverences her husband—that she notices him, regards him, honors him, prefers him, venerates, and esteems him; and that she defers to him, praises him, and loves and admires him exceedingly" (AMP).

Dave: Men, we have to understand that when our wives want to talk about "the marriage," they are not criticizing us. They want to feel connected and close, and talking does that for them. They are attempting to nurture the emotional side of the marriage.

Your wife is coming to you with her desire for connection. You need to welcome her. The best way you can do that is by listening and asking questions with the intent to understand. If you find yourself getting defensive, own up to it and express it by saying, "I'm feeling a little defensive right now, but I want to understand." Perhaps you need to take an emotional break and try again. If so, set a time to discuss it and show up. Empathetic listening takes time, but not as much time as clearing up misunderstandings.

First Peter 3:7 (NASB) states, "Husbands likewise, live with your wife in an understanding way." The verb "live with" is consistently translated in the Old Testament as "have sexual intercourse with." An "understanding way" implies acquiring knowledge and insight. Husbands, learn to listen to and be willing to be influenced by what your wives tell you.

The Triumph of Influence

Rather than using energy to battle and block each other's influence, we can use that energy to positively affect the people in our world. The most important work any of us has to do is found between the walls of our own home.

A tremendous bond develops over time as couples participate in joint projects, mutual goals, and creating a shared life. Our feelings for each other are enhanced by our passion about our shared projects. Raising children can be not only one of the most challenging, but also one of the most fulfilling projects we take on as a couple. We are changed by the experience.

"Biologically, adults produce children. Spiritually, children produce adults. Most of us do not grow until we have helped children to do so. Thus do the generations form a braided cord".[11]

Shared projects give a deep and lasting meaning to our relationship. As we work toward a shared purpose, we transcend and shape our emotional experience, and we solidify our relationship. President Jimmy Carter writes of his experience, "My wife has never been more beautiful than when her face was covered with black smut from scraping burned ceiling joists and streaked with sweat from carrying sheets of plywood from the street level up to the floor where we were working, cutting sub-flooring with a power saw, and nailing it down with just a few hard hammer blows."[12]

If you allow your mate's influence into your life, you will be transformed as a result. Each of you will feel an increased vitality and energy. You will have a more accurate picture of yourself and of your partner. You will feel a greater sense of worth, and you will be active initiators in your relationship and in your world. Because you feel more connection with each other, you will feel a greater motivation for connection with others.

As a couple chooses to be a positive influence together in their world, their marriage is transformed, and life pulsates through it. Boredom is no longer an option.

notes

Decision #ll
"I Will Allow You to Influence Me"

For Reflection and Discussion

1. Personal Evaluation: Read through the list of "exits" on page 197-198. Star the ways that you most often block your spouse's influence.

2. In your marriage, how have you allowed each other's influence? Are there ways that you have been transformed by love?

3. Complete these sentences.
"One of the ways I make it difficult for you to express your feelings is by . . . "
"One of the ways you can help me open up is by . . . "
Wives: Check yourself. Ask yourself, "Am I critical? Am I demanding? Is this issue something I can let go of?" (If you believe it is important and needs to be raised, can you turn it into a short, positive request?)
Husbands: Every day, give your wife one gift of verbally expressed feelings and thoughts. You be the initiator.
Wives: Receive your husband's gift. Respond to it with appreciation.

DECISION TWELVE

"I Will Work Through Issues with You"

> We were born naked, wet, and hungry, and then things got worse.

Life is full of challenges. Marriage is full of challenges. There are adjustments that must be made. There are conflicts that need to be resolved. There are values and beliefs that need to be reevaluated. There are issues that need to be faced.

Lesley Stahl of CBS's "60 Minutes" writes in her current memoir, *Reporting Live*, that she faced the greatest challenge of her life after her marriage in 1977. Her husband, writer Aaron Latham, was suffering from severe depression. Mike Wallace, her "60 Minutes" colleague who had suffered his own bout with the disease, persuaded her to get her husband to a doctor.

Stahl admits that her decision to stay with Latham was the thing that surprised her the most. "I was a great walker-outer," she explained. During one fight, she came as close as throwing her clothes into a suitcase and calling a cab. "He said, 'Stay and work this out. And in ten years you'll look back and say, I preserved this family,' " she writes.

"We talked. We cried. And we agreed to try," Stahl says. "Now it's nineteen years later and the thing I am most proud of."[1]

Abandoning our lifetime commitment to run into someone else's arms is the ultimate act of denial. One author expressed it this way: "Life is difficult. This is a great truth, one of the greatest truths. It is a great truth because once we truly see this truth we transcend it. Once we know that life is difficult—then life is no longer difficult. Because once it is accepted, the fact that life is difficult no longer matters."[2]

Once we stop railing against reality, we can redirect our energy toward facing the issues in front of us. Marriage can be a tremendous people-growing machine. A healthy marriage is not a marriage without issues that need to be faced. It is a marriage that has the backbone and commitment to face the issues that arise. These issues can provide the fertilizer for growth.

What are some of the issues married couples must meet? We can expect to face issues centering on the tasks of marriage, issues around predictable developmental stages, issues that result from the unpredictable curve balls of life, issues of polarization, and issues of personal preference. They certainly aren't all the result of being married; marriage sometimes just means having a friend by your side while you juggle the issues of life.

Tasks of Marriage

Separating from Parents

Diane and her mother have been joined at the hip ever since Diane's father deserted the family when Diane was thirteen. In fact, her adolescent years were spent emotionally parenting her mother. Now that Diane is married, her mother shows up whenever she feels like it, phones two or three times a day, and expects Diane to be her confidante. She has no other friends. Diane's husband, Rich, has questioned these intrusive actions. He is noticing how drained Diane is after yet another episode with her mother's neediness. He is upset that Diane's mother doesn't phone prior to showing up on their doorstep.

Diane has lost all objectivity. She sees Rich as critical and condemning of her mother. How could he be so cold? After all, Mother needs me. Diane is so loyal to her mother that she can't see mother's weaknesses as well as strengths.

Many couples that marry into a family with great financial reserves may find themselves almost blackmailed by their wealthy parents. If they don't come for dinner once a week, commit to spending every holiday with the parents, and raise their children following Mom and Dad's advice, financial privileges are withdrawn.

Other couples find that parents do more for them than one partner is comfortable accepting. Perhaps they are always arriving with unsolicited gifts, providing money to their adult child without the other partner knowing about it, or badmouthing the partner to their son or daughter. Regardless of the scenario, when one partner raises the issue of dissatisfaction with parental antics, the other one loses all objectivity and feels betrayed. "After all my family has done for you, how can you criticize them?"

Reliability Issues

Audrey was constantly upset with what she perceived as her husband's underfunctioning in their marriage. From her perspective, she was carrying all of the child-rearing responsibilities. Since she worked, getting everyone ready in the morning was her greatest challenge. She had asked Bryan to help her. Instead, he slept in until seven and then walked down the street to get a cup of coffee. He'd come back home by 8:15 so that he could drive the children to school. When he'd walk in the door, he'd comment on the frustrated tone that Audrey was using with the children.

Audrey would let Bryan have it, using a long string of criticisms and demands. Bryan could smell control a mile away, so he would resist. Both of them would attempt to force their personal solutions on each other rather than searching for a mutually acceptable solution.

Money and Time

When there isn't enough money or time, other issues raise their heads. Often the mate who earns the most money either spends more or believes that he or she should have the louder voice whenever financial decisions need to be made. At times the partner who makes the least will voice his or her frustration, "I'm fed up with having to ask for money like a dependent child," or they will in retaliation find alternative sources of income such as credit cards.

When one mate makes decisions about money without consulting the other, it almost always results in conflict. When two partners have different values about spending, saving, investing, or tithing time or money, problems arise. In those situations, the temptation is to attribute a "rightness" to your position and a "wrongness" to your mate's.

Cultural and Religious Issues

Jeff was raised in a "formal" church. He loves the traditions and the pomp and circumstance. He feels whole after attending church. Karrie joined a neighborhood Bible study, where she accepted the Lord as her personal Savior and began to read many books. Jeff is nervous that she'll turn into a "holy roller." When Karrie questions him about his faith, he gets defensive and then withdraws.

Issues rear their heads in marriages where one partner cannot make room for the other's traditions or beliefs. Instead of appreciating any breadth that can result in a relationship as a result of the other's uniqueness, the tendency is to become condemning and critical.

Parenting Issues

At each stage of their development, children present new challenges for parents. Different ideas don't need to threaten a marriage unless one spouse is rigid about the "rightness" of his or her way. If that partner won't allow the other to influence, and isn't open to discussion and learning to develop shared views (through counseling, classes, or books), the other will be frustrated.

Sometimes one parent is not willing to hear the other parent point out unhealthy choices that a child is making. This is particularly true in stepparenting situations, when a child gets in trouble. Sometimes partners turn on each other rather than joining forces to help the child.

Physical Intimacy

The issues that arise in the sexual area often have to do with differing ideas about frequency or what is acceptable sexual behavior. It seems as if sex is like air—it rises in importance when we feel we aren't getting any. When there are serious differences in this area, sex gains tremendous importance. Once again, if one partner insists on having his or her way, there will be painful issues to face.

Much heartache is caused when partners justify taking their sexuality out of the marriage relationship. Everything from porn to affairs, massage parlors, and Internet sex can tear a marriage apart.

notes

Drugs and Alcohol

This is a loaded issue. If couples differ about the use of alcohol or drugs, conflict will result. If one person has a problem and is in denial, the spouse will be left lonely and frustrated. If that partner attempts to intervene, and in the process of doing that, oversteps boundaries by attempting to control the other's choices, then other issues will also surface.

Weight and Appearance

Ralph would monitor how many times a week his wife would exercise and watch what she would eat. If she made a choice he didn't approve of, he'd be sure to point out her "sin." When she had her hair cut, he expressed his displeasure and withdrew for days. She deeply resented his intrusiveness and was learning to set boundaries, which created more issues.

Terrible pain is caused in marriages where a partner attempts to change or control the other's appearance. Issues also arise when one mate is careless about personal hygiene. Sometimes partners turn on each other because of age, injury, or illness. Each of these situations results in new issues for a couple to confront.

Issues around Predictable Stages

If, because of fear of conflict, you swallow your truth, you will become invisible to your partner. Your spouse will assume that you agree with him or her. It is crucial for personal and relational growth that both perspectives be brought to the table. Honesty will maintain your connection.

It's fascinating, because when you are honest or when you hear your mate's honesty, you may have conflicting emotions. You are learning more about your mate, but it isn't necessarily what you wanted to know. Your spouse's perspective can be threatening, frustrating, and extremely disappointing.

Jane felt those emotions when her husband told her that he

didn't want to have any more children. From his perspective, God had richly blessed them with their two children, and that was enough. Jane had been raised in a large family and desperately wanted more children. She wasn't exactly thrilled when he expressed how he was really feeling. It was an unsettling truth.

There is a somewhat predictable pattern that happens in a marriage when a couple confronts any new issue. It's as if the crisis forces the marriage through an hourglass. Perhaps you've been walking through your marriage with a sense of partnership and teamwork. You have seen eye-to-eye on many issues, and you feel comfortable. Then one of you wants something to change. Your anxiety mounts. It's as if you're being constricted into the narrow part of the hourglass. Your relationship doesn't feel comfortable. Your anxiety increases. Perhaps you are being asked to face something you don't want to face. It's unsettling. Who is this person you married anyway?

At this point you have four choices. You can try to force your spouse to accommodate you. If you do that, it's all about power and control and not about love.

A second choice is to swallow your truth and give in. At that point you stop existing in the marriage. You keep the peace, but at the cost of your individuality. When it becomes a pattern, this leads to an emotional and spiritual death.

A third option is to withdraw physically or emotionally from each other. At that point you become emotionally divorced.

The last choice is to grow up and learn how to mesh two people's uniqueness into a mutually agreeable solution. Together you create new options. You discover new resources. This takes time. In the process, you can't lose your thoughts, your nerve, or yourself.

As a couple discovers these new options, they come out of the hourglass on the other side stronger individually and as a team. They have come to a mutually agreeable solution that benefits both of them.

Some predictable crises that challenge us and force us into the hourglass are:

1. Separating emotionally from the family of one's childhood so as to invest fully in the marriage, while at the same time redefining the lines of connection with both families of origin.
2. Building togetherness by creating the intimacy that supports it, while carving out each partner's autonomy.
3. Embracing the daunting roles of parents and absorbing the impact of "Her-Majesty-the-Baby's" dramatic entrance. At the same time the couple must work to protect their own privacy.
4. Confronting and mastering the inevitable crises of life, maintaining the strength of the bond in the face of adversity.
5. Creating a safe haven for the expression of differences, anger, and conflict.
6. Establishing a rich and pleasurable sexual relationship and protecting it from the incursions of the workplace and family obligations.
7. Using laughter and humor to keep things in perspective and avoiding boredom by sharing fun, interests, and friends.
8. Providing nurture and comfort to each other, satisfying each partner's needs for dependency, and offering continuing encouragement and support.
9. Keeping alive the early romantic, idealized images of falling in love while facing the sober realities of the changes wrought by time.

(Adapted from Judith Wallerstein and Sandra Blakeslee)[3]

Issues around Unpredictable Realities

Many times a marriage confronts an adversity that knocks both partners off their feet. It feels like the end of life as they know it. It may affect their health. Perhaps it's an accident, a traumatic event, a child's death, illness, financial loss, or a failure that leads to losing the respect of one's peers. In these moments spouses need to be allies, not enemies. Once again they're forced into the hourglass, ready or not. There are issues to be faced.

Conflict around Polarizations

When one person makes his or her natural tendency "right" and at the same time looks at the spouse's pattern and perspective with contempt, polarizations are set up and power struggles result. One of the most familiar polarizations is the overfunctioner and the underfunctioner. Underlying the polarization may be the different sets of values that we bring to our marriages. We differ on what each sees as important.

If one partner fears change and needs lots of structure, and the other thrives on change and fights structure, another polarization is set up. Yet another polarization happens when one mate is more aggressive, dogmatic, and demanding. Wanting to attack problems directly, this partner often attacks his or her spouse as well. The spouse tends to avoid problems and ignore issues, giving in and giving up rather than confronting issues. In the process this person often takes on too much responsibility for the relationship.

One mate may operate primarily from an emotional orientation while the partner lives in the world of logic and action. Often men disown their feelings ("big boys don't cry") and women disown their perspectives in order to win the approval of one another. When this happens, the marriage suffers.

The last polarization that couples often need to contend with is the pursuer/distancer pattern. One person pursues connection, the other one pursues separateness. It's easy for the pursuer to push constantly for the relationship, but at the expense of other goals and life plans. Whenever you pursue, pressure your mate, or diagnose your mate's issues, you abandon yourself. The pursuer overloads the relationship. Often pursuing is an unconscious reaction to anxiety.

That is why this polarization often rears its head around significant transitions in the life of a couple: birth, wedding, job change, promotion, graduation, child leaving home, an ill parent, etc. It's easy and tempting to avoid your own anxiety by focusing on your spouse's issues. In order to bridge this great divide, the pursuer needs to become the spokesperson for more distance in the relationship, not because he or she is angry, but as a move towards meeting his or her own needs and goals. A wife who had been a pursuer said this to her husband: "I've been neglecting my friendships. I need to spend an evening with the gals. Could you tell me what evening would best coordinate with your schedule?"

A husband became the spokesman for greater distance when he said, "I need to go to the office and get some work done. I've been neglecting my job."

Issues of Personal Preference

These issues raise their heads when we want our spouses to "be like us." We disapprove of the way they look, act, or think. We become egotistical and in ways let our mates know of their inferiority. We try to force them into our box, and get angry if they don't do what we want. When we don't allow for individuality, we become condemning mates. This is a personal, spiritual, and emotional issue. We need to confront our attitude, our control, and our expectations.

Issues and Intimacy

The ideal relationship is built by two partners who are vulnerable with each other and who can define what they think, feel, believe, need, and want. We want to grow to be able to handle each other's discomfort with uniqueness, and not comply just to keep the peace. Time and support are necessary to grow into that kind of a couple.

A marriage needs many times of facing the constriction of the hourglass to come out of it with both mates respecting and valuing each other and respecting and valuing themselves. God has much to teach us through issue resolution. Rather than allowing ourselves to be torn apart, we team together to face whatever life sends. We don't cling to "your way" or "my way," but find the best way for us. "Love is the joyous conflict of two self-conscious persons who rejoice in one another's individuality and through the clash of mind on mind and will on will, work out an ever increasing but never finally completed unity".[4]

Attitudes and Issues

Is it natural for couples to always be thoughtful of each other, rarely struggle with impatience, and rarely get aggravated? Look at Christ's disciples. After three years of being mentored by Christ Himself, they were petty, competitive, and self-centered (Luke 22:24). So why should you expect your mate to always be a model of perfection?

The fact that you argue and at times get upset doesn't make your marriage a failure. In fact, in a landmark study on divorce, Amato and Booth (1997) found that seventy percent of divorcing couples were not highly conflictual. They avoided conflict instead of facing it. The study indicated that couples that divorced did not resolve conflict or rebound after a conflict.[5]

"For God did not give us a spirit of timidity," writes Timothy, "but a spirit of power, of love, and of self-discipline" (2 Timothy 1:7). In every problem-solving situation, God wants to give us those three gifts: love, power, and self-control. If any of these three gets out of balance, our ability to confront challenging issues will be greatly reduced.

Loveless Power

Imagine a continuum with power at one end and love at the other.

If, when confronting issues, we get off balance toward the power end, we move away from love. All we are concerned about is maintaining power. We see our position as "right." We want things our way. We outtalk, outdebate, or even manipulate our partners. We take any opposition as a challenge to come on stronger, with greater persuasion, until our mates eventually back down. Whether it is intended or not, this marriage is built with a hammer. This is the position we call Loveless Power.

Loveless Power comes from a self-centered, self-serving place, rather than a self-disciplined place. It is preoccupied with power, domination, and control. In Genesis 3, we are told that this is a result of the curse. Christ came to cancel the curse.

Needless to say, if you approach issue resolution with the attitude of Loveless Power, you may get your way—but at the price of your partner's self-esteem. One husband put it this way: "The day I finally realized I didn't need to control my wife—that indeed, I ought not to control her, that I couldn't control her, and that if I tried to, I would destroy our marriage—was the day our marriage began."

Powerless Love

Neither partner should feel that giving up an essential part of self is required to make the marriage work. If you have to sacrifice your voice and your will to appease your spouse, you have adopted the stance of powerless love.

Getting off-balance toward the love end of the continuum can be just as destructive to your "us" as leaning too heavily toward the power end. If you do this, you have allowed yourself to be taken hostage. You and your mate are not partners.

Does this paragraph describe you? You are loving, caring, giving, and sensitive, but you often feel powerless. You are terrified of conflict, so you do anything to avoid it. You often restrict your thoughts, words, and actions in order to maintain the status quo. You've disconnected from your vibrancy and spontaneity, because you take few if any personal risks. You're afraid to set boundaries, and you find it almost impossible to say no. Your theme has become peace at any cost . . . and what a cost it is.

Christian passivity, as well as a misunderstanding of Scripture, can keep you stuck in the position of Powerless Love. "I'm just waiting on the Lord . . . I don't want to get ahead of His timing," you may say. It can sound so spiritual, but it can result in a ticking time bomb in your marriage.

There are two sides to every argument until you take one.

When submission is defined as powerless love, we see submission as giving in and giving up, acquiescing and complying. You fit your spouse's image of what you should be, and in the process give up who God created you to be. Issues aren't resolved; you just adopt your mate's perspective.

Whatever we don't dare to confront becomes the North Star of our relationship. When we avoid issues and seek comfort at all cost, we are left without intimacy and compassion. Intimacy requires freedom, and intimacy requires honesty. Both honesty and freedom are missing ingredients in Powerless Love, so intimacy becomes impossible.

Partners in such a marriage go into hiding. We begin to feel smothered. We don't know the stuff of which we are made. We are like a chameleon changing its color to suit every situation. We don't know love, even if we pretend that our marriage is perfect.

Loveless Power and Powerless Love

Loveless Power attacks, withdraws, and attempts to win in every situation. From Loveless Power's stance, there is one "right" way and one "wrong" way to deal with every issue. Powerless Love, on the other hand, yields and withdraws when there are issues that need to be faced. One person simply acquiesces and swallows the partner's way.

When decisions are made by domination, the results don't reflect the concerns of both partners. Making decisions is adversarial rather than collaborative. We are left angry, depressed, anxious, and wanting to escape during an attempted problem-solving time. When domination is the pattern, we listen only for what's wrong with or what's missing in what our mates say. We feel like opposing sides in battle, rather than partners facing choices together. The result is fear, not love.

John and Jennifer rushed to the appliance store after work. They had three hungry children with them. They were exhausted and stressed out. Their microwave had died, and they needed to replace it. Jennifer pointed out the kind she liked. John completely ignored her suggestion and pointed out a cheaper one. Jennifer got caught up in a competitive exchange.

Instead of acknowledging John's financial concern and hearing him out, she started her next statement with a "but," which effectively minimized any concern John had. "But I don't want a microwave that is that small," she said.

John belittled Jennifer's input. "What do you know about microwave ovens?" he chided. "All you know is how to cook every meal in one of them." Jennifer falls for the criticism and reacts with complaints of her own.

"You never listen to anything I say," she says. "You're such a tightwad."

John lets her have it. "Well, someone has to worry about the finances. You're such a princess. And I guess that I'm just your money machine."

Jennifer is embarrassed. They are in an appliance store, and the tension is mounting. On one hand, she is glad that they are in a public place. If they had been at home, they'd be shouting now.

She tries to calm things down. "Well, I need a microwave, so let's get the one you want," she says. "I'll use my neighbor's when I find it too small."

"That's okay," he replies. "We can get the big one if you're going to act so immature and selfish. Go ahead and waste our money." Jennifer settles for the small one.

Loveless Power has had its way in their exchange. Both John and Jennifer have hurt feelings. They are frustrated because neither one of them feels heard. They've made a decision, but it doesn't embrace both of their concerns. Every time they use the microwave, they will remember the cruel comments and frustration of that night.

We think there is a better way. It is the way of Powerful Love.

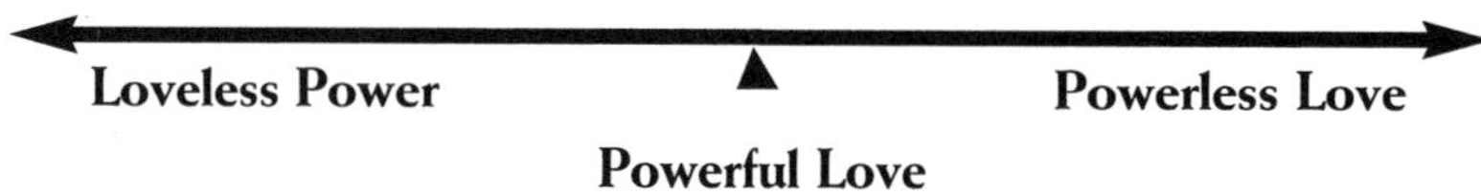

Powerful Love

Jesus is the only person in history who has balanced power and love perfectly. As the Apostle John told us, "Perfect love casts out fear." Often we don't even make Powerful Love our goal until we have experienced the pain, the fear, and the dissatisfaction of living in one of the other two extremes.

Powerful Love was evident in Christ's life. Even though He was God with all the power, He didn't relate to us from a one-up position. Jesus' leadership never dominated, demeaned, or demoralized people. The New Testament tells of Jesus leaving the power position at the right hand of the throne of God and coming down to earth alongside us, to love and to serve us. If anything, it was a "one-downmanship." He emptied Himself of all Loveless Power. But He didn't go to the other extreme of Powerless Love; His love didn't avoid difficult issues or difficult people. He demonstrated an incredible power balanced with an incredible love.

Christ initiated love, service, friendship, and forgiveness, but never did He force His will or His way on us. He didn't take away our freedom, our voice, or our decision-making. Just as Christ was the active servant committed to our best, so marriage partners need to be committed to each other's best. Paul puts it so clearly in 1 Corinthians 13:5, "Love is not self-seeking."

When we adopt the attitude of Powerful Love, we become interdependent, equal mates. Together we create a partnership. Our roles are based on our individual strengths. Decisions are made equally for the mutual benefit of the marriage. There are times when each of us is a follower (Ephesians 5:21). We each submit to the other's needs, and we give to and serve each other as Christ did. Rather than pushing our own way, we search for ways to effectively achieve our common vision and goals. We have a collaborative mindset.

Powerful Love Meets Issues

When an issue raises its head in your marriage, what is the result? If your attitude is one of Powerful Love, you and your spouse are allies facing problems together. You are dedicated to the solution being a win for both of you—a mutually agreeable solution. You are not threatened by one another's perspective. Just as it took the different perspectives of Matthew, Mark, Luke, and John to give us a more complete picture of the Jesus of the Gospels, it takes both of your perspectives to create an agreeable solution for whatever challenge or conflict you are facing.

Ralph and Barbara need a new microwave. Their old one has broken down. They are tired, hungry, and frustrated. They know better than to try to solve an issue when they are in that state, so they go home and eat some dinner. They arrange for the neighbor girl to come over and stay with their children. Then they start out to the appliance store.

Neither of them knows which microwave would best meet their needs. They decide to gather information together. Ralph asks Barbara to let him know what features are important to her. She says that all she really cares about is that it is large enough to accommodate her casserole dish since she uses it many times a week. Ralph is receptive to Barbara's input. He repeats her concern aloud, and then he expresses his concern about their financial situation since one of the children needs braces. He checks out a consumer guide for microwaves. Barbara reads it with him. She points out the one that doesn't need to be repaired as often. Ralph states that he would like the microwave to be the same color as their stove. Together they search for a microwave that fits both of their concerns. They leave pleased that they are such a good team.

notes

Steps to Issue Resolution

We have been influenced by Susan Heitler's ideas of collaborative problemsolving.[6]

- **Begin with a cooperative attitude.**

Diane and George approach issues of disagreement with a different mindset than

they used to. Previously they used to order each other around and announce to each other what they were going to do. They operated from a position of Loveless Power. There was no place for one another's input. They were caught in unilateral decisionmaking. Needless to say this often led to a power struggle.

Diane used to announce, "I'm going out with my friends tonight." Her words would take George by surprise, and her pronouncements would leave him feeling unimportant. Yet George's pattern was similar to Diane's. He'd say, "I'm playing on the church softball team tonight. You'll have to handle the kids on your own." At times his tone would be antagonistic. Diane would often react with some kind of sarcastic retort. No adult likes to be told that he or she has no choice but to go along with a mate's plan. No one likes to be left out of a team decision.

"Everyone must be quick to listen, but slow to speak and slow to become angry."

After attending a seminar on collaborative problem solving through work, George came home with a new perspective. He decided that he would approach Diane in a way that allowed her to have a voice in the decision. He said, "I would like to play softball tonight. Does that work for you? Is there anything I could do to lighten your load before I go?" What he discovered was that Diane's attitude made a 180-degree turn when he started involving her in the decision. She followed his example and changed the way she approached him.

- **Distinguish solutions from concerns**.

The year we were engaged, we lived 500 miles from each other. It was not a great way to do an engagement. We'd get on the phone and share our solutions to different problems with each other. Often, our solutions would be in direct opposition. Then we'd be battling over the "rightness" of our proposals. Our phone bills were astronomical, and our parents wondered if we really should get married.

It wasn't until we learned to really listen to each other's concerns—underlying preferences, desires, values, and fears—that we started to be able to resolve our differences. Concerns can have many solutions, not just one. Both partners' concerns need to be understood thoroughly before a solution is decided upon.

- **Express your initial perspective.**

Anna and Don were both in graduate school on the East Coast. Don graduated one year ahead of Anna and was offered the job of his dreams at a university on the West Coast. Don wanted to take the job and leave immediately. Anna wanted to stay in graduate school and complete her degree that spring.

- **Create a list of both of your concerns.**

In a loving marriage, when one partner has a concern, it becomes a concern of the other. Each makes it a priority to see to it that the other's concerns are taken seriously. Both are dedicated to this task, so they listen to understand each other's concerns. Together they make a list of our concerns, as opposed to yours and mine. The purpose of this list is to come to a double-win solution.

If in the process you find yourselves at an impasse, you are shifting into a right-way-wrong-way type of thinking. You need to stop and cool down, perhaps take a time-out to calm down, and then begin raising your concerns again.

You must guard against beginning with a specific solution in mind. That way you are open to explore options that best meet your underlying concerns.

Perhaps it would be beneficial even to spend an entire week looking at this issue from your mate's perspective. During this time, you need to act as if you want what your partner wants. Then you come together to discuss the issue again, expressing your partner's underlying concerns rather than your own.

Let's return to Don and Anna's situation. Her initial perspective: I want to complete my graduate degree. His initial perspective: I want this incredible job offer. Together they made a list of their concerns.

Anna: I'm concerned that if I stop, I won't complete graduate school.

Don: I'm concerned that if I don't take this job I'll never have another chance to work at this college.

Anna: It's important to me that you follow your dreams, and it's important to me that I follow mine.

Don: I couldn't agree more. I want you to finish your degree. I've always dreamed about the two of us team-teaching in a college setting.

Anna: So have I. In fact I've been concerned because I don't want this to tear us apart.

Don: I'm concerned about that, too.

- **Choose a mutually satisfying solution.**

"I could work on my dissertation anywhere once my topic is chosen and my committee has approved it," Anna said. "What I can't do is complete my courses anywhere else. I could finish them by Christmas."

Don offered to contact the college from which he had received the offer and to talk with the administration about their dilemma. He felt he needed to inform the administrator of their mutual commitment to see each other through graduate school. Anna suggested that they pray about it together on a daily basis.

After hearing about their commitment, the university administrator decided the college could wait until after Christmas for Don to begin his new position. Anna worked hard to complete her course requirements before lining up her dissertation committee. Together, they made plane reservations for Anna to come back to Florida two times to meet with her committee. In May she graduated, and there were two doctors in the family. Today they team-teach at that university.

This is the method that we find most beneficial in our own marriage. Yet it is certainly not the only way. Some couples agree ahead of time about who makes decisions in each area of their marriage. If a particular decision falls into one person's area of responsibility, he or she makes it. For example, the wife pays the bills and is responsible for the everyday functioning of the home. The husband may choose to do the grocery shopping and the cooking. Each can always seek out the other's input, but it is up to the one made responsible to make the final decisions in those areas.

This method works well if your values are similar, if you trust each other to follow through, and if you see the other as competent. Warning: Do not criticize each other's decisions after the fact. Give your input ahead of time, before the decision is made.

Some couples have a prior agreement to discuss the decisions in each one's area of responsibility before they are implemented. This gives the other partner the opportunity to give further input or to have veto power. For example, perhaps the wife is responsible for discipline, since she happens to be at home more than her husband. She shares with him that she is going to ban their daughter's TV and social outings for three weeks because she is not completing all of her homework assignments.

> "Intimacy requires a relationship that doesn't occur at the expense of the self and a self that does not act at the expense of the other."

Her husband reminds her of the youth program they wanted their daughter to attend. He asks if three weeks isn't too long, and suggests that he could take his daughter to his work setting after school for one week. There is an empty office there. She would have no distractions. She could have no TV or phone privileges until she showed her mother her completed assignments. His wife thought that was a great idea and informed her daughter of their decision.

Decisionmaking and issue resolution does not have to be painful. If you and your spouse are on the same team, and if your attitude is one of Powerful Love, then resolving issues can be an opportunity for shared creativity. When you collaborate, your decisions will generally be much more satisfying than your original ideas were.

Decision #12
"I Will Work Through Issues with You"

For Reflection and Discussion

1. How are you doing on each of these eight marriage tasks?

   Separating from parents
   Reliability issues
   Money and time
   Cultural and religious issues
   Parenting issues
   Physical intimacy
   Drugs and alcohol
   Weight and appearance

2. How do we make decisions? What is one mutually agreed-upon decision that we have made this past year? After reading this chapter, what adjustments might we like to consider in how we make decisions?

DECISION THIRTEEN

"I Will Forgive!"

> "Forgiveness can be the missing 'peace' in marriage relationships."

Ted distrusts Karen. The day before their wedding, when he was committing himself to Karen and her two children, she sat him down and told him that she had slept with five different men prior to dating him. He said he could have lived with this had he known about it earlier in the relationship, but to wait until the last minute made him question what else she wasn't telling him. He could not forgive her.

Scott and Shannon were struggling. She couldn't understand why he was so upset. She was showing him her new outfit when he blew a gasket about her spending $150. This made no sense to her since he had come home with a $1,000 set of Callaway golf clubs a few weeks earlier. He had also gone off to buy a new car and had returned with a much more expensive model than they had agreed upon. Then they had gone out to dinner with friends and he'd insisted on picking up the entire tab. She wondered why it was okay for him to spend money without consulting her, but it was not okay for her to do the same.

Both couples felt hurt and betrayed by their partners. In marriage, sometimes the hurt is caused by significant event. Other times, it's just a collection of seemingly small hurts that keep reoccurring. Unfortunately, these hurts can reduce the quality of our lives. The hurts can be like a poison that destroys our marriages.

Married people have been compared to two porcupines that lived in Alaska. When winter came and the snow began to fall, the porcupines felt cold and began to draw close together. When they drew close to get warm, however, they began to poke one another with their quills. When they separated, they became cold once again. They wanted to stay close, but they didn't want to keep getting poked.

The reality of marriage is if we let ourselves get close, we will be hurt from time to time. None of us is perfect. You are going to fail your spouse, and your spouse is going to fail you. Solomon spoke the truth when he wrote, "There is not a righteous man on earth who does what is right and never sins" (Ecclesiastes 7:20).

The disillusioned version of marriage is two stubborn people living together, getting on each other's nerves, and struggling through an emotional tug-of-war.

Wife: "I can't believe you forgot your own mother's birthday."

Husband: "Well, aren't you in charge of the calendar and sending out cards?"

Wife: "Don't blame me, she is your mother."

Husband: "Yes, but I told you last week to remind me, so why didn't you?"

Need we go any further! We can expect failure even from the people whom we love the most.

Hurt, pain, and suffering always produce a fork in the road. It is not possible to remain unchanged after encountering them. When you've been hurt, immediately you find yourself in the place of powerlessness. You did not expect this, ask for this, or deserve this. You are a victim of injury or injustice. You are one of the good guys, and your spouse is one of the bad guys. If that becomes your mindset, you become a permanent victim.

Some of us hate feeling powerless, so we react and swing to the opposite extreme of power and control, hardening our hearts and refusing to forgive. Since no one can make us forgive or force us to stop holding a grudge, we feel incredibly powerful, which helps compensate for the original feelings of powerlessness. With that mindset, we set out to inflict as much pain on our partners as they have inflicted on us. If our only choice is to hit the other person as hard or harder as he or she hit us, then we are part of the problem.

When we choose to stay victims or choose to get revenge, our wounds become more important than our relationships. Our hearts are hardened, and bitterness is the result. The only thing more harmful than hurt is bitterness. If we choose bitterness, we focus on the hurt more than on developing the health of our relationship. Bitterness keeps pain alive!

Understanding Forgiveness

We all have memories of our mates expecting too much or too little. There were times when they were overbearing, distant, unaffectionate, absent, or hurtful. At other times, they may have used hurtful labels to describe us, or misperceived our motives. In anger they may have berated or belittled us.

The purpose of forgiveness is to let go of the pain and get on with our life together. Forgiveness makes us feel whole, helps us like ourselves, and rids us of the excess emotional baggage that weighs us down. Forgiveness stops the past from interfering with our lives and happiness in the present.

Jan: I travel alone when I go to speak at women's conferences. I carry my own baggage as well as my book boxes, which can be cumbersome and tiring. A few months ago, I was met by a group of couples when I got off the plane, instead of the usual women. The men carried all my bags. When I got up to speak that evening, I was shocked by how much energy I had. When I tried to figure out the reason, I realized that lifting heavy bags and boxes has drained my energy at past conferences. In the same way, resentment and bitterness are heavy baggage . . . but we don't realize it until we stop carrying them. Forgiveness helps relieve the burden we carry.

The choice to release our hurt and forgive is a long, difficult, and even painful journey at times. When we have been deeply hurt, the normal human response is to be unloving and unforgiving. We find ourselves thinking, Wait a second, I'm the injured party here. Why should I do all the work? Why should I forgive? He should be apologizing to me.

For many, forgiveness is equated with:

Giving up
Giving in
Wimping out
Admitting defeat
Forgetting
Absolving
Condoning
Letting the "bad guys" get away with the rotten things they did
Releasing a tidal wave of frightening emotions
Reliving unpleasant experiences
Leaving one vulnerable to being hurt again

Sometimes by not forgiving we feel we are punishing the one who hurt us. Our anger may be hot or cold. We might attack or say nothing.

Forgiveness alone can halt the cycle of blame and pain, breaking the chain that imprisons us. Forgiveness gives our relationship new life. If we are going to understand clearly what forgiveness is, then we must first of all understand what it is not.

Forgiveness is not ignoring our pain.

If we do so, we close ourselves off from all feeling. **Dave recalls:** When I was growing up in Canada, I loved to ice skate and play hockey. We had a pond about a quarter-mile from our home that would freeze over. Many times as a child, I can remember staying out in the cold far too long. There were times when my hands would become numb. I can still remember coming home, taking off my boots, gloves, and coat, and going over to the floor registers, where the heat came up from the furnace in our basement. As my hands would begin to thaw out, I would start to get a painful tingling in my fingers—as if needles were pricking me. I remember thinking it would be less painful just to go back outside. When my hands were numb, I didn't feel any pain.

In a similar way when we have been hurt, so often we want to numb our pain. As we begin the process of forgiveness, we start to feel negative, painful feelings.

Forgiveness is not denying our pain, pretending it never happened.

It is not just smiling and saying it is all right when it isn't.

Forgiveness is not pushing our real feelings under the surface.

Did you ever try to push a beach ball under the water and hold it there? If you have, you know how hard that was to do. The deeper down you tried to push it, the harder it was to control. You thought you had it under control, only to have it dart out in an unpredictable direction. Similarly, if we are trying to push our hurts under the surface, then we should not be surprised if they pop out when we least expect them to.

Forgiveness is not minimizing our pain.

We say, "It's no big deal," when it really is. It was bad. It did hurt. It has made a difference in our life. Nothing is gained by minimizing it.

Forgiveness is not forgetting.

We don't forget short of a frontal lobotomy. There are always emotional consequences to face.

Forgiveness is not denying your spouse's responsibility.

It is not letting our partner off the hook or letting the bad guy win. Each person is responsible for his or her actions and needs to face the reality of the pain caused.

Forgiveness is not instantaneous.

It is not like a light switch that you just turn off and on. It's a process that takes time. We do a disservice to ourselves if we believe that forgiveness is a quick and easy process.

Forgiveness is not reconciliation.

It takes only one to forgive; it takes two to reconcile.

It is so important to address these misconceptions. If we ignore, deny, minimize, or try to forget the injury, it's as if we are putting a Band-Aid on a deep, cancerous wound that needs surgery or radiation. Forgiveness is hard, hurts, costs, and is a process.

Forgiveness is an essential part of an intimate relationship.

Underlying Foundation for Forgiveness

Jesus provides our foundational example for forgiveness. We forgive because we have been forgiven. In Matthew 18:23-25, Jesus tells the parable of the unforgiving servant. Because of the servant's huge outstanding debt, the king ordered him to be sold along with his wife, children, and all their possessions. The servant pleaded with the king, who showed compassion and released him from his financial indebtedness.

After experiencing the king's forgiveness, the servant turned around and went after one of his fellow servants who owed him a minor amount of money. When this other servant pleaded for more time, the forgiven servant showed no mercy, but had him thrown into prison. When the king was told about this, he was furious. He delivered the forgiven servant to his tormentors until he paid the debt in full.

Jesus cut to the chase when He said that if we don't forgive we cannot expect forgiveness. In the Lord's Prayer, we pray, "Forgive us our trespasses, as we forgive those who trespass against us." If we are not forgiving, then we are telling God He doesn't need to forgive us.

Undertaking Forgiveness

Dave: Several years ago I went into a Christian bookstore and saw a display rack of a newly released book. The title caught my attention: *Caring Enough Not to Forgive*. My first thought was, What is that book doing in a Christian bookstore? My curiosity got the best of me, so I began paging through the book. I wanted to understand where the author, David Augsburger, was coming from.

As I scanned the book, I suddenly came to a page that was upside down. It looked as if the publishing company had really blown it. I turned a few more pages, and they were all upside down. The whole second half of the book was upside down! I closed the book to look at the back cover only to find another front cover, which said *Caring Enough to Forgive*.

In a creative way, this author summarized the two major stages of true forgiveness.[1] If we embrace both of these stages when we've been hurt, we will experience a new maturity and our marriage relationship will benefit. We will discover what it means to be powerful lovers in the forgiveness process. Let's look at this two-stage process for releasing hurt.

Stage 1: I care enough not to forgive until:

I've recognized and released the misconceptions I hold about forgiveness.

Previously, we have addressed possible misconceptions about forgiveness. To summarize, forgiveness is not:

a. Ignoring our pain

b. Denying your pain and pretending it never happened

c. Minimizing your pain

d. Forgetting

e. Denying your spouse's responsibility

f. Instantaneous

g. Reconciliation

I have honestly revealed the impact of the injury to my spouse.

You must deal in reality and not try to escape from what really happened. You have to let go of any of these misconceptions and be honest with your spouse about how he or she hurt you. You must admit that you have been hurt, and in what ways. Let's not be dishonest or superficial. Let's not pretend.

Bob blew it big time and got sexually involved with another woman. Kay found out and confronted him. She insisted that they see a counselor. He discounted that idea, telling her that he never meant to have an affair. He was sorry and said, "Just forgive me, and let's put it behind us. I don't even want to talk about it. It will just hurt you more if we talk about it. Let's just go on from here."

Kay was not satisfied with sweeping this under the carpet. She insisted they see a counselor, which he eventually agreed to. In the counselor's office, Bob again expressed his remorse, but when Kay started talking about her pain, he got upset. "Why do you keep bringing this up?" he asked. "If you were as good a Christian as you say you are, you'd just forgive. I don't want this thrown in my face for the rest of my life. I told you, I'm sorry."

Kay was afraid to let him know how hurt and angry she was because he might use it as an excuse to go and see the other woman again. On the other hand, she asked the counselor, "What do I do with all these feelings? I can't go on pretending they aren't here."

The counselor gave her permission to be honest.

Looking directly at her husband, Kay began to let the pain out. Through tears she said, "From the point I found out about the affair, it was as if a knife pierced my heart. It took the life out of me. I never dreamed that you, Bob, of all people, could hurt me in this way. I haven't been able to sleep since I found out, and I've completely lost my appetite. When I do try to eat, I throw up. Every time I see you look at another woman, I feel inadequate. When I'm undressing in front of you, I feel compared. When you are making love to me, I wonder if you are thinking about her or really present with me. I find myself obsessed with getting the details, and yet another part of me doesn't want to know anything more. I'm tempted to become a private investigator, but I don't want to lower myself to be constantly checking up on you. My trust has been devastated, and my dreams for our marriage are shattered. The fact that you did this while I was carrying our child leaves me repulsed. I can't look at the baby without being reminded of your affair."

Kay had more to say. "To make you comfortable, I'm supposed to quickly forgive and go on as if nothing happened," she said. "That is stupid and shortsighted. We'll both lose. I can't just smooth this over when all these feelings are raging inside of me. Frankly, it feels like I am being set up. What happens in a year or so when some beautiful woman puts a move on you again? If you have no idea how deeply your choice devastated me, and you are tempted again, will you just rationalize and act out? For a moment you might think, *Kay was very upset, but she got over it fairly quickly. It's worth the risk.*"

notes

Kay's honesty in revealing the depth and intensity of her hurt, even though it made Bob feel guilty, bad, and like a loser, will act as a deterrent to him in the future. The memory of her agony will provide a reality check the next time he is tempted. He will remember and think, I don't ever want to see Kay suffering like that again, so I won't give in and violate her by having another affair.

How shortsighted it would be for anyone to pressure Kay into a quick, phony forgiveness. It is imperative that the one who has been hurt is given time to feel and express that hurt. That process always takes time—considerable time if the injury is severe. When that is the case, we would like to suggest that you write a letter in which you disclose to your partner the full intensity of your hurt, anger, and pain. By first writing your pent-up feelings in this form, you give yourself and your spouse an opportunity to hear and acknowledge hostile feelings in a structured, safe manner.

When writing such a letter, you must allow yourself to progress through each emotional level: expressing your anger and resentment; your hurt, disappointment, and pain; your fear, anxiety, and insecurity; your sadness, remorse, and responsibility; your wishes, specific goals, and wants (not your demands); and your love, understanding, and forgiveness. (Expressions and phrases that can help you articulate all these levels are given at the end of the chapter.)

Obviously, one is not going to take the time to write a heart letter for the little irritations and resentments of life, but we have found this to be a beneficial exercise when there has been a major hurt in a marriage. It gives couples a chance to start anew.

When dealing with a major hurt, there comes a point in the process when continuing to rehearse the pain becomes detrimental to the injured spouse. It is then that we must move on to the second stage.

Stage 2: I care enough to forgive.

Jesus put it this way, "If your brother sins, rebuke him, and if he repents, forgive him" (Luke 17:3). We must move to take this second major step in the process, and come to the place that we care enough to forgive. This kind of forgiveness is not superficial, quick, or shallow.

An affair is an extreme example of our need to forgive. What do we do, however, about the little irritations and day-to-day hurts? Sometimes we need to just forget them and let them go. Perhaps your husband forgot to pick up the dry cleaning, or your wife didn't mail a letter. Maybe you had planned to meet each other at a restaurant at 6 p.m. and one of you was late. If this isn't a pattern, let it go. Don't ruin the entire evening.

One time we were going to meet each other at a fast-food restaurant. We each had one of our kids with us. Each of us went to the agreed-upon restaurant, but in different parts of the city! We waited and waited. Finally we realized what might have happened, so we hopped into our cars to drive to the other McDonald's in town. Would you believe that we passed each other on the way? We had to laugh and let it go!

If the irritation is small but still needs to be dealt with, then set a time to let your partner know that you are upset. Don't let the irritation fester until it becomes something major.

No failure is larger than grace. If forgiveness is in the picture, nothing in a relationship has to permanently destroy that relationship. No hurt exists that love cannot heal. But for all these miracles to take place, we must be willing to be part of the solution, not just part of the problem.

Forgiveness is an act of the will. It is our prayer that you will choose to make forgiveness an ongoing part of your relationship. True forgiveness is:

Letting go of the intense emotions attached to past incidents

Recognizing that you no longer need your resentments, hatred, and self-pity

No longer wanting to punish your spouse

Accepting that nothing you do to punish your spouse heals you

A byproduct of becoming whole
An internal process
A sign of positive self-esteem
A way to free up and use your energy more effectively
The only way to move onward and forward

True forgiveness involves letting go.

Two monks living in the Philippines vowed together to abstain from all earthly temptation. They both understood that this meant that they would never have contact with females. It was a lifetime vow, and for decades they had kept it.

One day as they walked back to the monastery, it began to rain, and the streets were transformed into muddy canals. As the monks approached an intersection, a young girl in a beautiful white kimono stood helpless, unable to cross to the other side of the road. One of the monks impulsively picked her up and carried her there.

The other monk was furious. They walked in silence until they came to the gate of the monastery. Finally the angry monk could contain himself no longer. Reminding his brother monk of his promise, he pointed out how blatantly he had broken his vow by carrying the young girl across the road, and he demanded an explanation.

The monk who had carried the young woman replied, "I put her down back there on the road. You're the one who still seems to be carrying her!"

Undermining Forgiveness

You will know forgiveness is complete if you can begin honestly to renew your love with your spouse. Sometimes we say that we forgive, but quickly move on to attack and demean the one who has hurt us. Other times we offer forgiveness, but then we accompany the offer with a number of conditions.

John and Judy sat before us in the office. Fifteen years before, Judy, who was not a Christian at the time, had had an affair. It was a one-night stand. She felt terrible about it and confessed it to her husband. Since her confession, she had tried to do everything possible to meet his needs and make things right. No matter what she did, he refused to forgive. He constantly brought up the affair and used it to manipulate her. He refused to let it go. He claimed that he had forgiven her, but his actions and attitude betrayed his words.

We must learn to truly forgive. Our health and happinessdepend on it. Let's choose to follow Christ's example and do the following:

Release the minor irritations
Resolve the major hurts
Overthrow our hatred
Renew our love
Rekindle our friendship
Continue to grow

Each of us needs to stretch ourselves beyond our bitterness, our fear, and our solitude. As we face the disappointments and hurts of life, our love can be strengthened.

Decision #13
"I Will Forgive!"

For Reflection and Discussion

1. Check the following general ways in which you are feeling hurt by your spouse:

Disappointment
Rejection
Abandonment
Ridicule

Humiliation
Betrayal
Deception
Other:

2. What is your natural response when your partner hurts you or lets you down? How did you learn to respond in this way?

3. How do I know if I have truly forgiven my spouse? Answer the following questions with a yes or a no.

Do I hold grudges or harbor bitter or resentful feelings?
Do I find myself treating my partner as I was treated growing up?
Do I feel empty inside?
Have I built walls between us, leaving me feeling lonely, isolated, and alienated?
Do I find it hard to let myself get close to my partner?
Do I approach new challenges expecting to be disappointed?
Do I keep track of my partner's wrongdoings?
Do I revisit the list of wrongdoings when we have an argument?
Am I on guard most of the time so I won't be hurt?
Do I feel incomplete?

If you marked "yes" to two or more of these, it is likely that you are still hanging on to something that once hurt you. Unfortunately your past is still reverberating in your present.

4. Write a heart letter to your partner. The following lead phrases may help if you have difficulty moving from one stage to another.

Level 1: ANGER—Express your anger and resentment:
"I hate it when . . . "
"I'm disgusted with . . . "
"I'm angry about . . . "

"I'm fed up with . . . "

"It's devastating to me when you . . . "

Level 2: HURT—Express your hurt, disappointment, and pain:

"It hurts me when . . . "

"I felt betrayed when . . . "

"I feel disappointed that . . . "

"I feel rejected when . . . "

"I feel jealous when you . . . "

Level 3: FEAR—Express your fear, anxiety, and insecurity:

"I feel scared when I . . . "

"I am frightened when you . . . "

"I'm afraid that . . . "

"I feel tense and anxious when you . . . "

"I feel insecure about . . . "

Level 4: SADNESS—Express your sadness, remorse, and responsibility:

"I'm sorry that . . . "

"I feel awful when I . . . "

"I feel sad that I . . ."

"I feel sad that you . . ."

"I feel guilty because . . . "

Level 5: WISHES—Express specifically your wishes, goals, and wants, not your demands:

"I would like for us to have counseling sessions with a competent therapist . . . "

"I wish I felt . . . "

"I wish you had . . . "

"I want . . . "

"I hope . . . "

Level 6: LOVE and FORGIVENESS—Express your love, understanding, and forgiveness:

"I love you because . . . "

"What I love most about you is . . . "

"Thanks to this relationship I . . . "

"I'm proud of you for . . . "

"I forgive you for . . . "

"I forgive myself for . . . "

"I love it when . . . "
"I understand that . . ."
"What I have learned is . . . "
(adapted from Harold Bloomfield)[2]

5. Perhaps you are reading this chapter and you aren't carrying any hurts, but you are aware that you have hurt your spouse. What do you do now? Why not list the ways you know you have hurt your partner recently?

What do you do if you are carrying some resentment because of ways you have been hurt? Make a list of the ways that you have been hurt.

6. Share your lists with each other and ask forgiveness. Then as a sign of letting go of the hurts, burn your lists. Together read Matthew 6:14, 15 and pray as a couple. Here is a sample prayer you might find useful.

Dear God,

I am willing to totally forgive what has been talked about today, as You have already forgiven me. I release my spouse into Your keeping. When the memories of these hurts return, I will remember that You have forgiven me, and I will not hold resentment against my mate.

Help me process my resentment. Help me to take daily spot checks, and when I am wrong, or when I am wronged, help me to own it.

I admit my own shortcomings and accept Your loving forgiveness for all the selfish, unkind things I have said or done. Thank You, Jesus, for giving me my spouse, and thank You for all the pleasure, comfort, and happiness we bring to each other.

Thank you for Your presence with us. Amen.

EPILOGUE

"I Will Become the Change I Seek"

But Jesus said, "Not everyone is mature enough to live a married life. It requires a certain aptitude and grace. Marriage isn't for everyone. Some, from birth seemingly, never give marriage a thought. Others never get asked—or accepted. And some decide not to get married for kingdom reasons. But if you're capable of growing into the largeness of marriage, do it" (Matthew 19:11–12, The Message).

Each of us must master the ordinary. Just as a pianist's competency depends upon consistent practice of scales and arpeggios, the health of a marriage depends on its partners making the same thirteen intentional choices day after day.

Marriage isn't all about chemistry. That is a great place to start, but in order for a relationship to thrive, two people have to exert daily conscious effort, decision, and choice.

Your choices allow you to weather any storm that threatens your marriage. In the crisis, you can stand firm and continue to make the same thirteen choices you made prior to experiencing the fury of the storm. Choice can sustain and even create emotion as you weather tough times.

The Apostle Paul writes that good things come out of difficulties. "Suffering produces perseverance; perseverance, character; and character, hope" (Romans 5:3,4). Notice that Paul placed hope at the end; hope emerges from the storm as a byproduct of faithful perseverance in the important choices.

We need to look at our marriages with a long-term view. Are the choices we are making in the moment going to strengthen or threaten our love?

A thriving marriage is created by two partners who hold hands while they make the tough choices to go forward step by step, moment by moment. With each step they discover that the ground on which they are standing is becoming more solid. Love works that way.

Daily CheckUp

Have I locked the escape hatch and thrown away the key?
Am I intentional about my marriage?
Do I make our relationship a priority?
Do I revisit my expectations regularly?
Do I champion my spouse?
Do I nurture my private life?
Am I a reliable and responsible partner?
Am I honest?
Am I choosing to connect?
Do I reveal myself to my spouse?
Do I allow my partner to influence me?
Do I work through issues with my partner?
Am I willing to forgive?
We must become the change we seek.

We love being married to each other!
We love the challenge of it
The pain of it
The agony of it
And the exhilaration of it.
We are both capable of living alone
YES
But what companionship, what fun
and
What accountability for growth
Would be lacking in our lives.

Through personal struggle and introspection
We have learned
That only as we love Christ more
Than we love each other
Do we have enough love
To love each other with.

We have learned that feelings of love flow
As a result of intentional daily choices.
We become life mates for a lifetime
As a result of embracing all facets of each other.

But embracing only each other leads to isolation
And despair
For we have discovered our need to be surrounded
By other couples
Who love Jesus and who love us,
Who are committed
To love us, to be honest with us, to support us, and
To challenge us
In times of joy
And times of despair
When we experience their embrace
Christ's love infuses our lives
and
Revolutionize our marriage in ways we
Didn't ever imagine.

For information about Dr. David and Janet Congo's books, tapes, resources, and speaking engagements, contact:

Dr. David and Janet Congo
23441 S. Pointe Dr., Suite 180
Laguna Hills, CA 92653
Telephone toll-free (949) 859-5937 or
call (949) 452-9294
Web site:www.elifemates,com.com

ENDNOTES

DECISION 1

[1] Philip Yancey, *Reaching for the Invisible God*, (Grand Rapids, Michigan: Zondervan, 2000), 271.
[2] Linda Waite and Maggie Gallagher, *A Case for Marriage: Why Married People Are Happier, Healthier, and Better off Financially*, (New York: Doubleday Publishers, 2000), 78.
[3] Ruth Harms Calkins, *Marriage Is So Much More, Lord*, (Wheaton, Illinois: Tyndale, 1979), 33.
[4] Neil Clark Warren, *Triumphant Marriage*, (Colorado Springs, Colorado: Focus on the Family Publishing, 1995), 37.

DECISION 2

[1] Eric Fromm.
[2] Yancey, *Reaching for the Invisible God*, 92.
[3] Ibid., 183–184.
[4] From a story by Joan Curtis, *Flint River Review 96* (Albany Writers Guild, P.O. Box 72174, Albany, GA 31708).
[5] Judith S. Wallerstein and Blakeslee, Sandra Blakeslee, *The Good Marriage*, (New York: Houghton Mifflin Company, 1995), 205.
[6] H. Norman Wright, *So You're Getting Married*, (Ventura, California: Regal Books: Ventura, California, 1985), 65–66.

DECISION 3

[1] Terry D. Hargrave, *The Essential Humility of Marriage*, (Phoenix, Arizona: Zeig, Tucker & Thiesen, Inc., 2000), 6.
[2] Steve Covey, A. Roger and Rebecca R. Merrill, *First Things First*, (New York: Simon & Schuster, 1994), 89.

DECISION 4

[1] *Wall Street Journal*, March 29, 1999.
[2] Judith Wallerstein, *The Unexpected Legacy of Divorce: A 25 Year*

Landmark Study, (New York: Hyperion, 2000), 112.
[3] Garrison Keillor as quoted in *Reader's Digest.*
[4] Bill O'Hanlon, *Do One Thing Different*, (New York: Quill, Harper Collins, 2000).
[5] *Time*, Aug. 28, 2000.

DECISION 5

[1] Bob Burg, as quoted on www.smartmarriages.com.
[2] John Powell, from lecture on Unconditional Love.

DECISION 6

[1] *Fortune*, April 3, 2000.
[2] Leo Buscaglia, *Loving Each Other*, (New York: Fawcett Columbine, 1984), 197–198.
[3] Gordon Dahl, *Work, Play, and Worship in a Leisure-oriented Society*, (Minneapolis: Augsburg, 1972), 12.
[4] Kahlil Gibran, *The Prophet*, (New York: Knopf, 1923), 16.

DECISION 7

[1] Keith Korstjens, *Not a Sometimes Love*, (Waco, Texas: Word, 1981), 71.
[2] Jacobson & Margolin, 1979.
[3] *Marriage Partnership*, Fall, 2000.
[4] Hoehschild, 1989.
[5] Thoits, 1992.
[6] Hargrave, *The Essential Humility of Marriage,* 111.
[7] John Gottman, *Why Marriages Succeed or Fail*, (New York: Simon and Schuster, 1994), 17.

DECISION 10

[1] James Farmer quoted by Ralph McGill, *Atlanta Constitution*, April 24, 1968, 1.
[2] David and Amy Olsen, *Empowering Couples:Building on Your Strengths*, (Minneapolis, Minnesota: Life Innovations, 2000), 24.
[3] *Redbook*
[4] Cloud, Henry and Townsend, *Boundaries in Marriage*, (Grand Rapids, Michigan: Zondervan, 1999), 71.

DECISION 11

[1] Sam Horn, Tongue Fu, (New York: St. Martin's Griffin, 1996), 129. (Norman Cousins quote.)

[2] Carrie Chapman Catt, 1902.
[3] Harville Hendrix, *Getting the Love You Want: A Guide for Couples*, (San Francisco: Harper and Row Publishers, 1985), 107.
[4] Thomas Jones, from letter written to the authors.
[5] Rachel Naomi Remen, M.D., *Kitchen Table Wisdom*, (New York: Riverhead Books, 1996), 220.
[6] Philip Yancey, *The God Who Is Invisible*, p 111.
[7] *Redbook*, July, 1997.
[8] David Seamands, *Reflections in Clergy Couples in Crisis*, (Carol Stream, Illinois: Leadership Library, Word, 1985), 144–145.
[9] *Los Angeles Times*, John Wooden story (Saturday, October 24, 2000), C-12.
[10] Terry Hargrave, *The Essential Humility of Marriage*, 11.
[11] George F. Will, *Washington Post*, as quoted in *Reader's Digest*.
[12] Jimmy and Rosalynn Carter, *Everything to Gain*, (Fayetteville: The University of Arkansas Press, 1995), 92.

DECISION 12

[1] Lesley Stahl, *Reporting Live*, (New York: Simon and Schuster, 1990), 57.
[2] Scott Peck, *The Road Less Travelled*, (New York: Simon and Schuster, 1978), 84.
[3] Adapted from Judith Wallerstein and Sandra Blakeslee.
[4] From a paper by G. A. Studdert-Kennedy, as presented at Smart Marriages.
[5] From a paper by Amato and Booth, as presented at Smart Marriages.
[6] Susan Heitler, *The Power of Two*, (New Harbinger Publications, 1997), 20.

DECISION 13

[1] David Augsburger, *Caring Enough to Forgive*, (Ventura, California: Regal Books, 1981), 69.
[2] Adapted from Harold Bloomfield, M.D., Sarah Vetlese, Ph.D., and Robert Kory, *The Love Fitness Program for a Lasting Relationship*, (Markham, Ontario: Penguin Books, 1989), 165-170.

Other LifeMates Resources Available at your local Christian Bookstore or contact us at 800-323-7543 or www.cookministries.com.

Dates for Mates

Romancing the One You Love

By Lisa Keyes and Debbie Black

Learn from real-life stories of the different ways that couples are molding their date life into the circumstances and stages of their marriage to keep romance alive. Couples will find inspiration and practical, fun ideas for bringing romance back into their marriage.

ISBN: 0-78143-690-7 $14.99 Retail

They Call Me Mr. Romance

A Business Man's Guide to Romancing Your Wife

By Michael Keyes

Sometimes hard-edged, sometimes hysterical, Mike Keyes tells it like it is (and was) in his own straight-talking, no-nonsense style. This is no ordinary marriage book — Keyes lays out his life, mistakes and all, revealing a successful business man who could close multi-million dollar deals at the office, but still somehow miss the mark at home. . . that is, until he became "Mr. Romance."

ISBN: 0-78143-691-5 $12.99 Retail